Merry christmas
from Martin & Chris
1986

HEARST CASTLE
SAN SIMEON

HEARST CASTLE
SAN SIMEON

Text by Thomas R. Aidala   Photographs by Curtis Bruce

FOREWORD BY WILLIAM RANDOLPH HEARST, JR.
INTRODUCTION BY DAVID NIVEN

HARRISON HOUSE

New York

TO OUR PARENTS

Marianne and Vincent Aidala / Curtis B. Bruce and Lucy M. Bruce

EDITOR AND PUBLISHER: *Paul Anbinder*
COPY-EDITOR: *Harriet Schoenholz Bee*
DESIGNER: *Betty Binns Graphics/Betty Binns*
COMPOSITION: *U.S. Lithograph Inc.*

Manufactured in Hong Kong

Library of Congress Cataloging in Publication Data
Aidala, Thomas.
    Hearst Castle, San Simeon.

    Reprint. Originally published: New York: Hudson
Hills Press, 1981.
    Bibliography: p.
    Includes index.
    1. Hearst-San Simeon State Historical Monument
(Calif.)   I. Bruce, Curt.   II. Title.
F868.S18A33   1984   708.194′78   84–15722
ISBN 0–517–460823
h g f e d c b

Frontispiece: The Neptune Pool at Hearst Castle, San Simeon.

Contents

*The Main Terrace fishpond is the setting for one of San Simeon's
loveliest sculptures, "Galatea" by Leopoldo Ansiglioni.*

Foreword

I WAS 11 years old when I first saw the site on which my father had chosen to build his dream. It was only three months after his mother (our beloved "Grandma Hearst") had died.

My mother and father, their guests, and my brothers and I lived in United States Army surplus tents from World War I, which dotted the hilltop along with the wood and canvas sheds that housed scores of workmen, while my father supervised the building of the circular concrete retaining walls for the guest houses, the first structures to be completed.

The building went on for some 30 years until shortly before my father's death in 1951. The entire complex at San Simeon stands today as one of the world's most visited tourist attractions and as a lasting tribute to the imagination and genius of William Randolph Hearst and to his frail little genius of an architect, Julia Morgan.

Now, in this appealing and brilliantly illustrated book, the fantastic amount of thought, time, and effort my father expended in the construction of San Simeon is successfully brought to life. Tom Aidala has done a fine job of depicting both the period and the principal participants in this tremendous project, and Curt Bruce's photographs have added to his work a wonderful new dimension.

I trust that my gratitude and pleasure in this fine publication will be matched by that of others.

W. R. HEARST, JR.

View from La Cuesta Encantada of the coastal plain at the lower end of the Hearst Ranch.

Introduction

AMONG the happiest and most rewarding times of my life were those I spent as a guest at the "ranch," William Randolph Hearst's Enchanted Hill.

My favorite memories of those days are of the elk herds grazing in the surrounding hills or of Hearst on a horse in full regalia leading us to some remote spot for a picnic, or standing, unmoving, in the center of the tennis court like a magnet and whacking back everything that came within his long reach!

They are fond memories, indeed, and it was my great good fortune to have been able to enjoy the splendor and hospitality offered at San Simeon. Thanks to the Hearst family bequest of the Enchanted Hill to the people of California, everyone can now follow in my lucky footsteps and enjoy this most remarkable of places. And, for its further enjoyment, I find this fascinating and beautifully illustrated book a must for all who would venture there.

I particularly appreciate how well Hearst's love of animals is portrayed, although I would add here a particular remembrance of the time when he was told that the mice in the kitchen had to go, and only agreed provided they were caught unharmed in traps. These he then emptied in the garden and the happy little creatures hotfooted it back into the kitchen for their next meal!

His love was, of course, not so great for politicians, who now have their hands on the takings from the many visitors to San Simeon and only allow a small proportion of it to filter back up the hill to help pay the enormous maintenance.

This instructive and honest book also at last gives Julia Morgan her due for all she did toward building this extraordinary place.

Reading the book made me homesick! It also made me furious that when I was there I did not have it with me to make my enjoyment of the place even greater!

DAVID NIVEN

*Visitors arriving by car from the south first see the Castle among the
rocky promontories of Hearst Ranch land.*

Preface and Acknowledgments

MANY VISITORS to San Simeon bring with them opinions of William Randolph Hearst based on the motion picture *Citizen Kane*, on the dimly remembered editorial positions of his newspapers, on the many books written about him, or, more often, on some fragment of the historical residue that remains of so protean a man. Such opinions cannot help but color how the buildings and grounds are viewed.

One of the purposes of this book is to separate prevailing opinions about Hearst's life from what he and his architect Julia Morgan built at San Simeon. The subject is not Hearst or Morgan but the Enchanted Hill and the roles they played in shaping it. The brief history of Hearst's life is included only to provide a context for the Enchanted Hill.

In any nonfiction account there are bound to be certain facts about people and events that are unclear or contradictory. That is true in this book, and unavoidable, since the event was a process that began in 1919 and continued for some 28 years. A number of the people who played roles on the Enchanted Hill are still alive; many have died. Fortunately, some of those who either participated in the building or were guests at San Simeon have recorded their reminiscences in taped interviews. Because of the distance between the time of the interview and a person's participation in an event or part of the process, in some instances around 40 years, it is possible that certain recollections are not quite accurate. For the most part, there has been a surprisingly high degree of coincidence in people's remembrances about certain events and about the characters of Morgan and Hearst.

Many of the people involved, particularly Hearst and Morgan, also left behind abundant written records. The Hearst papers in The Bancroft Library at The University of California, Berkeley, and the Morgan papers at The California Polytechnic State University, San Luis Obispo, contain thousands of letters, speeches, telegrams, and other documents; unfortunately, these have not yet been fully inventoried. It is in these papers that the bulk of the correspondence between Hearst and Morgan is to be found.

Most of Julia Morgan's documents relating to the construction of San Simeon were removed from her office in two large trucks by the Hearst Corporation after her death; but the corporation has lost track of the final disposition of those papers.

The documents presently on the site are a catchall of what was there when the state of California took custody and what is occasionally donated—drawings, some records relating to the collection, sales and purchase slips, and so on. Most of these, too, remain uncatalogued with the exception of those relating directly to the collection.

The story in this volume, while incomplete in detail, provides an outline that will familiarize the reader with the progression of events that led to what can be seen today. We do not pretend to have delved deeply into the monumental amount of material available; such a task would require many years of full-time scholarship. But we have attempted to correct certain of the more egregious misconceptions about the place, misconceptions which had been accepted as fact because of constant repetition, and perhaps shed some light in a few dim corners.

Those interested in Hearst's life are directed to the many books written about him, especially *Citizen Hearst* by William A. Swanberg.

The absence of photographs of the interior of House C (Casa del Sol) is conspicuous and regrettable. The house was extensively damaged by a bomb explosion in February 1976, and reconstruction and restoration were incomplete while this book was in preparation.

Among the persons interviewed, three individuals employed at San Simeon were particularly helpful: Taylor Coffman, Historical Guide; Ann Miller, Park Maintenance Supervisor; and Norman Rotanzi, Head Groundskeeper.

We would especially like to acknowledge five persons without whose help this book probably would not have been completed.

First, we wish to thank William Randolph Hearst, Jr., whose enthusiasm for the project matched ours. The time he devoted, his critical opinions and help with the manuscript, the stories he told, and the assistance he offered when it was needed were a source of amazement, considering the extent of his other commitments.

Opposite: The carefully planned picturesque siting of Casa Grande and its adjoining buildings as seen from the coastal plain west of the Enchanted Hill.

Jerry Fialho, Area Manager, Hearst San Simeon State Historical Monument, gave us all manner of assistance and offered complete access to the buildings and grounds.

Ann Miller, whose title understates her efforts to maintain the collection, was not only a mine of information but also unlocked doors to hidden riches when no door was apparent.

Susan Ann Protter encouraged us from the beginning and rode the roller coaster of this project with us all the way.

Finally, Taylor Coffman, since 1972, has been quietly and diligently establishing the provenance of the entire collection. His work will ultimately establish it in scholarly relationship to other collections of the period as well as emphasize its uniqueness. Taylor checked the manuscript for accuracy, answered questions, and was completely free with the invaluable fund of information he has developed. He was also kind enough to write the captions for the photographs.

Early in his remarkable career, William Randolph Hearst entertained the notion of becoming a photographer. Although his interest in picture-taking subsequently waned, he is reported to have shown serious ability toward the craft. Curiously, there seems to have been relatively little photographic documentation of the Enchanted Hill during the years in which Hearst was in residence there. And, during the 23 years of the state of California's custody of San Simeon no serious attempt has been made to photograph the environment as a whole.

The challenge of documenting what must be America's most unusual private residence proved to be rather monumental: more than 20 visits over a period of more than two years were made during the course of location photography, resulting in a vast quantity of photographs. Linhoff, Hasselblad, and Nikon equipment was used; the film was made by Kodak; and the black-and-white pictures were printed on Agfa Brovira paper. In addition to the many friends who contributed to this enormous undertaking, special thanks are due Denise Evans Ferry.

We want also to thank those whose patience was tried by our absences: Rita and Tania Skevos and Mary Letterii.

Further thanks are offered to Marion Wheeler, who first took a chance on us and on the book, and who supported the project after she no longer had a commercial interest in it.

Others who helped in one way or another are the California State Park staff at San Simeon; Paul Anbinder, Alec Briones, Lindy Brown, Cliff Coulston, Dan Danks, Martha Deese, Hoyt Fields, Will and Nan Hearst, Dave Highland, Glenda Highland, Betty de Lancellotti, Jim MacKenzie, Carolyn Martin, John Melvin, Judy Olivier, Connie Rowley, Ken Sayre-Peterson, Suesan Sayre-Peterson, David Seidlitz, Barry and Beverly Silberstang, Sarah Smith, Monica Suder, and James Woodruff.

Invaluable assistance in the photographic documentation of the Enchanted Hill was provided by Sara Holmes Boutelle, Robert Hillman, George Hoffberg, Phillip MaKanna, George McGinnis, Ellen McNeilly, and Arthur and Virginia Robbins. Special thanks are due Peter Perkins, the lighting and technical consultant.

The site plan of the top of the hill is used with the kind permission of the office of Theodore Osmundson and Associates, Landscape Architects, which produced the drawing. The floor plans of Casa Grande were drawn by Kathrin Moore.

THOMAS R. AIDALA
CURTIS BRUCE

HEARST CASTLE
SAN SIMEON

WILLIAM RANDOLPH HEARST
AND JULIA MORGAN

 THE FIRST EUROPEANS to settle on the American continent almost five centuries ago were the Spanish. For years their way of life prevailed in much of the New World. In the United States, that early influence is still felt strongly in the Southwest and California. One of its particularly visible aspects is in an architectural style common to those regions. Similarities of climate, land-forms, and available building materials between Spain and California have reinforced the appropriateness of the derived Spanish style of building, despite the vast cultural and political changes that have occurred in both places.

The Spanish arrived in Alta California in force in 1769. Gaspar de Portola, governor of Baja California, commanded a military expedition whose purpose was to make an exploration of California by land and sea in an attempt to establish a strong Spanish presence that would blunt Russian incursions south along the coast from Alaska.

The securing of that presence was realized by the emplacement of military settlements at San Diego, Santa Barbara, Monterey, and San Francisco along with the establishment of 21 missions from San Diego to Sonoma, north of San Francisco. Each mission was granted a substantial tract of land stocked with good trees for lumber, good soil for growing foodstuffs, and a plentiful, easily obtained supply of water for drinking and cultivation.

Opposite: View of San Simeon from the approach drive.

In 1822, after 12 years of sporadic violence, the Mexicans and Californians finally liberated themselves from Spain's colonial rule. One of the immediate goals of the Mexican revolutionary government was to dilute the power of the church and to obtain church lands. In 1831, secularization was enforced in California by the governor of the province, José Maria Echeandia. The mission lands were divided and redistributed through grants among the loyal influential Californians who had fought for independence. The Mexican government issued 809 grants to individuals totalling 13,000,000 acres of California's most fertile land.

In 1846, the United States and Mexico went to war over the entry of Texas into the Union and the desire of President Polk to acquire, by any means, California and New Mexico. The conflict ended in 1848, with Mexico forced to cede most of what is now the southwestern states. The status of the 13,000,000 acres of prime California land would not be decided until the latter half of the 19th century, after years of legal skirmishes.

San Simeon and environs: detail of a map of San Luis Obispo County, 1899. Courtesy California Historical Society, San Francisco.

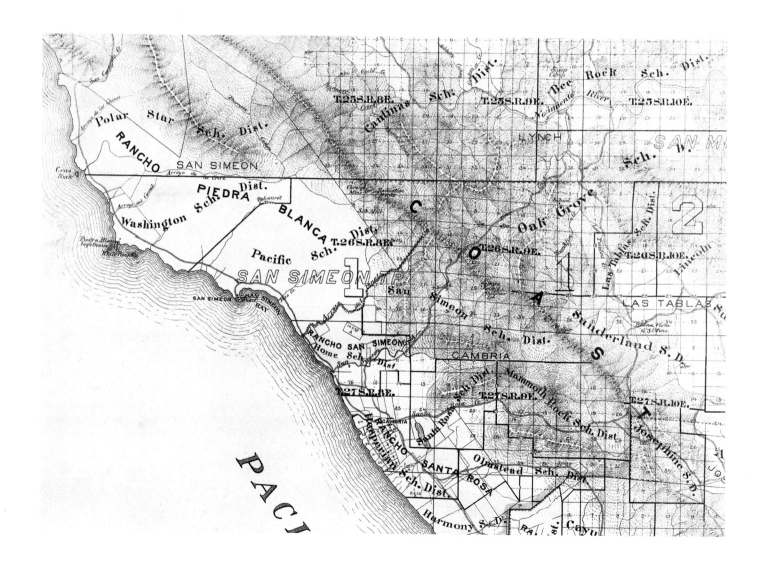

Thirteen years after his acquisition of the Piedra Blanca ranch, George Hearst built this 18-room house in a grove of trees near the beach. The structure is still used today by the Hearst Corporation.

One of the men who ended up with some of it was George Hearst. His first entry into the California land sweepstakes was the purchase of the 48,000-acre Piedra Blanca ranch from José de Jesus Pico. It was the nucleus of what was to become the 270,000-acre Hearst San Simeon ranch. Years later, when George Hearst's son William Randolph Hearst began to build a home for himself on this tract of land on the California coast it was not inappropriate that it would ultimately be Spanish in style.

George Hearst had arrived in California in 1850, chasing gold. He is described in all accounts as an honest and ingenious man who had obtained the rudiments of mining skill by working in the local lead mines close to the family farm in Franklin County, Missouri. With only two years of formal schooling behind him, he had slowly and grudgingly read a few books on mining and geology, which, on the basis of subsequent events, it appears he thoroughly mastered.

It took him nine years to find and coax his first fortune from the ground. With the earnings from that first mine on the Comstock ore vein Hearst bought himself a one-sixth interest in what was to become one of the richest mines in the country, the Ophir mine outside Auburn, California.

George returned home from California in 1860, a very rich man, after receiving word that his mother was ill. For two years he personally tended his mother and also met and courted Phoebe

Left: George Hearst. Right: Phoebe Apperson Hearst. Both courtesy California Historical Society, San Francisco.

Apperson. Phoebe, a slip of a woman barely five feet tall, had already taken control of her life by becoming quite educated by frontier standards; a school teacher, she spoke not only impeccable English but French as well. She was 19, he 41. She was small, well-mannered, with a hunger for culture; he was a kind, handsome, large, strong, hard-working, whiskey-drinking, tobacco-chewing man, a gambler with a vocabulary.

On June 15, 1862, after his mother died, Hearst and Phoebe Apperson eloped and were married; then they journeyed to San Francisco by a rich man's route—train to New York City, boat to Panama, train across the Isthmus, and then another boat to California. In San Francisco on April 29, 1863, Phoebe Apperson Hearst gave birth to her first and only child, William Randolph, named after his grandfathers. It was on their journey to California that Phoebe and George met Mr. and Mrs. David Peck and their two-year-old son Orrin. The families would remain friends the rest of their lives, and Orrin would become one of William Randolph Hearst's few close friends and the painter of the portrait of Hearst that hangs in his study at San Simeon.

The dominant factor in Will Hearst's childhood was the care, pampering, and love in which his mother encapsulated him. The former schoolteacher was determined that her son be as well educated as possible, and so she undertook the task herself. She supervised his childhood carefully and indulgently, insisting that he learn but allowing his every whim.

Coming from a semifrontier where access to the arts was severely limited, she plunged herself into the cultural life of San Francisco in the 1860s, such as it was. With George gone most of the time, Phoebe undertook her own cultural education in order that Will might more directly receive his. She studied the humanities and the fine arts; she attended the theater and opera and visited private galleries. She also opened her house to artists and scholars, a practice she would continue all her life.

While Phoebe was smothering her only child in motherly love, George was out striking a fortune from the ground as miraculously, it seemed, as Moses struck water from the rock. He had developed, as well, a passion for land, and in 1865, the year he was elected to the California state legislature, he bought the Piedra Blanca ranch.

In 1873, Phoebe took Will and his tutor on his first trip to Europe. The ten-year-old Hearst, rather than becoming bored and irritated by the endless travel, the wandering for hours through art galleries and museums, castles and antiquarian shops, was genuinely enthusiastic and stimulated, absorbing it all. He had penetrated the world of art, delighted in its pleasures, and was taken with it for life. They stayed a year that first trip, and while wandering through Europe, Will was tutored in French, German, English, drawing, and arithmetic. He also started a collection of his own: German comic books.

In 1879, Phoebe decided to enroll Will in St. Paul's School in New Hampshire to prepare him formally for entry into Harvard in 1882. But the 19-year-old Hearst and Harvard were just not made for each other. He shared too much of his father's frontier attitude toward convention—he simply had no use for it—to accommodate himself to an institution and city that elevated social convention to a high art. Though not an intellectual in the academic sense, he possessed, nonetheless, a first-rate mind and a powerful ability to concentrate. He was, however, an indifferent student and was given more to practical jokes than studies.

Hearst's first job in journalism was as business manager of the *Harvard Lampoon*. He plunged into the job with a vigor usually reserved for his pranks. He had a keen skill, it turned out, in orchestrating promotional schemes as well as increasing the paper's income. At this time he began studying other publications: the *Boston Globe*, whose offices he frequently visited, and Joseph Pulitzer's *New York World*, which he loved for its radical departures in what was then a largely conservative business. More importantly, Will began to look critically at the *San Francisco Examiner*, which George Hearst

*Orrin Peck, a close friend of the Hearst family, painted this portrait of
William Randolph Hearst in 1894, when the publisher was 31 years old.*

had acquired in 1880. Will Hearst found the *Examiner*, compared to the fiery *New York World*, graphically unattractive, poorly edited, poorly written, and poorly illustrated. He became convinced something should be done about it.

Will was suspended from Harvard in 1884 after financing a wild celebration of the victory of President Grover Cleveland. The event reached its climax when dozens of roosters were set free in Harvard Yard, awakening and enraging both students and faculty. He decided to pass the time of his suspension in Washington, D.C., observing the political process. His mother was also in Washington, preparing a house for George and herself, and no doubt preparing Washington for George, who, it was understood, would be appointed senator as soon as the ailing incumbent from California died.

It was from Washington that Will wrote his father asking for the *Examiner* for the first time: "I have begun to have a strange fondness for our little paper . . . a tenderness like unto that which a mother feels for a puny or deformed offspring, and I should hate to see it die now after it had battled so long and nobly for existence; in fact, to tell the truth, I am possessed of the weakness which at some time or another of their lives pervades most men; I am convinced that I could run a newspaper successfully. Now if you should make over to me the *Examiner* . . . with enough money to carry out my schemes . . . I'll tell you what I would do!"[1] He went on to discuss those things which he believed needed to be done to make the paper successful and demonstrated that he had already acquired a substantial understanding of Pulitzer's style of newspaper publishing.

He returned to Harvard the following spring but was finally expelled in his junior year in 1885, at the age of 22, after having had delivered to his instructors chamber pots elegantly inscribed with their names. George offered his son his choice of properties to manage—the Barbicora ranch in Mexico, the Anaconda mine, the Homestake mine—but Will had his mind set on journalism. He had taken his own measure and decided he was going to excel in the newspaper business.

He went to New York and took a job with the first newspaper he had loved, the *New York World*. His intent was to learn all he could about journalism. He noted its rise in circulation and studied its curious mix of outrageous sensationalism and intense idealism. Importantly, he learned that penny papers could make millions. While he was receiving his real education at the *New York World*, he continued his campaign to convince his father to give him the *Examiner*.

In 1886, upon the death of California Senator John T. Miller, George Hearst cashed in his political chips and was appointed to complete Miller's term. The following year he was elected to a six-year term. He finally made over the *Examiner* to an enormously jubilant, self-confident, and eager son.

Will had his newspaper before he was 24 years old. He had his dreams and ambitions for that newspaper and the energy to realize them. It would take time and money, time that Will had and money that George had. Three years after Will took over, and after he had poured $800,000 of his father's money into the paper, the *Examiner* made its first profit.

George Hearst died at the age of 70 on February 28, 1891. Out of regard for the abilities of his exceptional wife and probable lack of regard for Will's abilities where money was concerned, he left his entire estate and his son's care to Phoebe's unfettered management, "in full confidence that she will make suitable provision for him." Four years later, after listening to Will's constant requests for a large loan, she sold her interest in the Anaconda Copper Mining Company and gave Will the proceeds of the sale, $7,500,000. William Randolph Hearst was now ready and able to begin serious expansion of his journalistic and artistic activities.

In 1895, he bought the *New York Morning Journal*, a newspaper as somnolent as the *Examiner* had been. At the *Examiner* and the *Journal* he invented most of today's circulation-boosting and journalistic techniques, along with a style and approach that made a story thrilling and compelling to read, if not always entirely accurate.

He discovered that earth-shaking events do not happen daily, even if circulation demands that they do, and that it was often necessary to create those events out of the commonplace, even to create them out of nothing. He became a master at ballyhooing the trivial and, in the process, invented the non-event. He used lurid headlines and illustrations, and was the first publisher to put photographs on the front page. The *Journal* never achieved any literary or high journalistic distinction but it did sell.

In his battle to gain preeminence over the established New York papers, he was prepared to spend millions of dollars. He distributed mounds of sweaters and gallons of free coffee to the city's unemployed. He set up soup kitchens for the indigent, rained a blizzard of posters upon New York, strung banners everywhere, entertained with bands, and generally informed New Yorkers that the *Journal* was under new management. "Putting out a newspaper without promotion," he once said, "is like winking at a girl in the dark—well intentioned but ineffective."[2]

He raided the *New York World* and other competing newspapers and bought their top talent, including R. F. Outcault, the popular cartoonist of "The Yellow Kid," a strip about a street urchin. Pulitzer was furious over Outcault's defection and took Hearst to court. While the case was being adjudicated, Pulitzer hired another cartoonist to continue drawing "The Yellow Kid." New Yorkers were amused that two newspapers of a similar lurid persuasion both carried strips called "The Yellow Kid," a situation that led to the term yellow journalism. Hearst eventually won the case and rights to the strip.

Late in 1895, Hearst discovered the cause of a small band of Cuban rebels fighting for independence against an enfeebled Spain. For the next two years both the *Journal* and the *World* engaged in what can only be called creative writing. Cuban battles that never occurred were described in bloody detail. Tales were told, with accompanying illustrations, of women's humiliations at the hands of the Spanish brutes. Rallies and torchlight parades of thousands were organized in New York to pledge common cause with the rebels. Hearst sent two eminent men to Cuba, reporter Richard Harding Davis and artist Frederic Remington. Remington telegraphed from a placid Havana to a seething New York: "Everything is quiet. There is no trouble here. There will be no war. I wish to return. —Remington." Hearst's reply has since become famous: "Please remain. You furnish the pictures and I'll furnish the war. —W. R. Hearst."[3] Hearst and Pulitzer spoke out passionately to the country for war; they promoted war and finally were successful.

What was not lost on Hearst, or on Pulitzer, was that if one could create a war it was just possible to get anything one wanted through journalism. In 1899, Hearst announced the Hearst American Internal Policy, advocating public ownership of the public franchises that were then controlled by the trusts, such as the railroads, the telegraph, and possibly the mines. Hearst also called for the election-at-large of United States senators so that they could be more responsive to the will of the people rather than serve as the purchased instruments of industry. He called for a graduated income tax (which he would fight against in later life) and for the establishment of a universal public school system.

In his only successful bid for public office, Hearst won a seat in Congress from the 11th district in New York. He served from 1902 to 1904 and at best was a diffident congressman. He ran for mayor of New York in 1905 as an independent and lost by a whisker. Democratic Tammany Hall, it was rumored, dumped thousands of his votes into the East River. Although he lost, Hearst emerged as a kind of popular hero and certainly a contender for the 1906 gubernatorial race against Charles Evans Hughes. He ran as a Democrat, but the party machinery in New York City turned against him again, and he lost—the only Democrat running on the ticket to do so.

In 1908, he made an unsuccessful attempt to get the Democratic nomination for the presidency. He finally repudiated the Democratic Party and fashioned the Independent Party, which nominated two Hearstians, Thomas Hisgen and John Graves. The election results

William Randolph Hearst in the Refectory at San Simeon.

were a disaster. Hearst candidates polled only 87,000 votes nation-wide. Without a home in the Democratic Party and unable to convince the electorate of the viability of his own party, even with the force of his newspapers behind him, he had no place else to go in politics, although he did continue to attempt to influence and guide both nominating conventions and elections.

His greatest success occurred in 1932 during the Democratic con-vention when, by phone and telegraph from his perch at San Sim-eon, after hours of convoluted political maneuvering, he was able to swing the nomination to Franklin Delano Roosevelt. There are many ironies in Hearst's securing Roosevelt's nomination. A number of social programs for which Hearst had fought years before would be enacted into law by Roosevelt but, by then, Hearst had come to disagree with many of them. The greatest irony, of course, is that the promise of the avoidance of foreign entanglements made by Roosevelt to secure Hearst's support during the convention would have to be broken during Roosevelt's time in office. Yet it was precisely World War II that saved Hearst's publishing empire after he had nearly spent it into ruin by the end of the 1930s.

Hearst's personal affairs were often as intense and convoluted as his professional and political enterprises. On April 28, 1903, one day short of his 40th birthday, he married the beautiful Millicent Will-son, a stage dancer whom he had met some six years earlier. On April 10, 1904, the Hearsts had the first of their five sons, George, named after both grandfathers. In 1907, William Randolph, Jr., was born, followed in two years by John Randolph. In 1915, twin boys were born, David Whitmire and Randolph Apperson.

Marriage did not appreciably alter the pattern of Hearst's life. He would still attend the musicals and revues that he loved, have a late supper, work on his newspapers, and retire early in the morning. He also spent an increasing amount of time and money in the New York art galleries and auction houses.

The Hearsts first lived in a four-story brownstone house on Lex-ington Avenue and 28th Street that he had bought in 1900 and which was starting to fill with part of his growing collection. They decided, after the birth of William Randolph, Jr., that it was just too small for a family of four. In 1907, they rented the top three floors of the 12-story Clarendon apartment building on Riverside Drive. Their apartment contained thirty rooms, but in only ten years Hearst decided it was too small for them. He proposed that the owner evict the tenants on the eighth and ninth floors, and, by including his tenth floor, create a vast three-story space. The owner balked, so Hearst bought the building for around $1,000,000 and proceeded to construct for himself the largest apartment in the nation.

By 1919, the year he started planning his residence at San

Millicent Willson Hearst in 1903. Courtesy California Historical Society, San Francisco.

Simeon, Hearst had decided that he would become a film producer and make Marion Davies a national film star to rival Mary Pickford. Hearst approached movie making with the same fervor that characterized his other endeavors. He left nothing to chance, no detail personally unstudied. He bought an old amusement center at Second Avenue and 127th Street in New York and rebuilt it, making it the finest movie studio in the nation. The Hearst Cosmopolitan Movie Studios housed, at various times, such idols as Ramon Novarro, Gloria Swanson, and Lionel Barrymore, but it was clear to everyone that the movies made there were primarily vehicles to propel Miss Davies to stardom.

Marion Davies had been discovered by Flo Ziegfeld, who put her into the 1917 production of his Follies, and it was about this time that she and Hearst met, probably through Ziegfeld. By all accounts, she was a kind, lovely, talented, and extremely witty young woman who possessed an infectious, bubbling enthusiasm. Hearst hired the best tutors, writers, and directors to mold her still rough talents and inundated the public with stories about her. Her movie openings became news events, emblazoned in headlines on page one of his newspapers throughout the country. Hearst spent abundant sums of money on the movies he made. In an era when $100,000 could buy an extravagant film, Hearst, it was rumored, spent $1,500,000 on *When Knighthood Was in Flower*, starring Miss Davies, which was a critical success.

Marion Davies. Courtesy The Museum of Modern Art, New York/Film Stills Archive.

Hearst's involvement with the film industry and with Miss Davies lasted for the next three decades, until his death. During that time he entered into an association with Louis B. Mayer of Metro-Goldwyn-Mayer Pictures. His studio operations in New York were too far away from both his home at San Simeon and the studios in Los Angeles. Since he did not want to travel excessively, he folded his Cosmopolitan Productions into M-G-M, which agreed to finance his films, give him a share of the profits, and pay Miss Davies $10,000 a week. The quid pro quo was that the Hearst press would pay considerable attention to all M-G-M productions.

Marion Davies became the object of his adulation and devotion, one of that quartet of remarkable women whom, for different reasons, he would respect and love throughout his life. His mother, Millicent (the wife who would never divorce him), Marion Davies, and his architect Julia Morgan were the people to whom he was most courtly and, in his own way, most friendly. He also allowed these four to penetrate his shy reserve and offered to them as well his curious brand of fidelity, a trait not particularly apparent to those who worked for him on his newspapers.

Hearst's mother was one of those remarkable people who possessed genuine compassion, which manifested itself as strength of character rather than as social obligation. Quite soon after arriving in San Francisco she had begun making discreet inquiries after talented and gifted children of poorer families and quietly arranged money for their education. She established kindergartens for the children of the working poor in San Francisco, Washington, D.C., and at the locations of her husband's mines. She was active in the movement to provide housing for displaced and lonely working girls, helping to establish the YWCA and expand its areas of operation. She helped found the Traveler's Aid Society and was instrumental in the birth of the PTA. Believing profoundly in the value of education, she spent a great deal of time as a regent of the University of California, trying to establish that institution as a quality center of learning. She had earned the reputation (along with Mrs. Leland Stanford) of being the largest educational donor in the United States, her gifts to the university totalling around $10,000,000. She was also active in founding Mills College for Girls in Oakland, California, as well as in providing countless young women with opportunity and money, support and encouragement.

In 1896, Phoebe Hearst was approached by Bernard Maybeck, an eccentric, talented architect then teaching in the College of Engineering at the University of California, Berkeley, with the idea of holding an international competition for a physical plan that would make the scruffy young Berkeley campus the "Athens of the West." Appreciating the social importance of the proposal, Phoebe Hearst agreed to fund the competition. Bernard Maybeck then set out to stir the interest of European and American architects, encouraging them to participate in the competition.

Maybeck and his wife made a number of trips to Europe, always visiting Paris, home of the École des Beaux-Arts, then the finest school of architecture in the world and Maybeck's alma mater. Paris was, as well, the home of his former student, the precocious, Oakland-born Julia Morgan.

In 1899, Phoebe Hearst, on a visit to Europe, met with Maybeck to confer about the rules and structure of the competition. Maybeck was staying at Julia Morgan's home, and while there Mrs. Hearst met the young woman whose life she was so profoundly to affect.

Julia Morgan was born on January 26, 1872; she was nine years Will Hearst's junior and like Phoebe Hearst, was frail looking and barely five feet tall. She was to become one of the most influential architects in America and certainly the most important woman architect in the world.

Fall 1890 found Julia Morgan, at 18 years of age, one of two dozen women enrolled in the University of California, pursuing a higher education at a time in which such an activity was viewed as a wholly masculine prerogative. In her sophomore year, Morgan decided to study architecture, a career she had long considered, influenced both by her cousin, Pierre le Brun, a prominent architect practicing in New York, and by her family's unconventional attitude toward Woman's role in society.

Since the University of California did not offer studies in a school of architecture, she enrolled in the College of Engineering, the first woman ever to do so, much to the chagrin of the students and faculty. While she was there she met Bernard Maybeck, who had practiced architecture in New York, Florida, and Kansas City, and finally settled in Berkeley as a drafting instructor at the College of Engineering. At his home, he held private classes in drawing and other architectural skills for those students whose real desire was the study of architecture.

Julia Morgan joined those classes immediately upon Maybeck's urging, and it soon became apparent to him that she was someone very special. Morgan, on her part, was exhilarated by the brilliance of his skills and ideas and the lyrical world of architecture to which Maybeck introduced her.

Julia Morgan. Photograph c. 1927–28; courtesy Sara Holmes Boutelle, Santa Cruz.

In 1894, Julia Morgan was graduated from the College of Engineering, the first woman to receive that degree from the university. Talented and clever as she was, proficient as she had become, it was clear to both Maybeck and Morgan that her education was only half complete. She would have to study architecture more thoroughly, especially that part that had been neglected in the School of Engineering: planning, the design of buildings, the disposition of space, mass, light, and decoration. Maybeck insisted there was only one place where she should study and that was at the École des Beaux-Arts in Paris.

Only a few years earlier the Beaux-Arts had dropped its restrictions against foreign students entering for study. The faculty was therefore shocked when a foreign *female* student arrived and applied to take the difficult entrance examination. Never expecting to be confronted by the possibility of a woman entering its halls, the school had no specific restriction against women. Still, it was the 19th century, and the administration was quite candid with Morgan. It told her that even if she succeeded in entering she would never receive her diploma, much less practice architecture.

Morgan persisted. While Maybeck lobbied for her with friends at the school, she started a program of private study to prepare for the examination. She studied French intensely, mathematics constantly, and drawing in her free time. After two attempts she was allowed to take the exams and passed—13th among 392 competitors. Julia Morgan became the first woman ever to enter the Beaux-Arts.

It was during this period that Phoebe Hearst met her and was impressed by the young woman's struggle against the incredible prejudice at the Beaux-Arts. Knowing she could use some assistance, Mrs. Hearst made her an offer of financial aid which Morgan graciously rejected: "If I honestly felt," Julia Morgan wrote to Phoebe Hearst, "more money freedom would make my work much better, I would be tempted to accept your offer—but I am sure it has not been the physical work which has been, or will be the hardest part, for I am used to that and strong but rather the months of striving against homesickness and the nervous strain of examinations. Now that my brother (Avery) is here, and a place is won at the Beaux-Arts, really mine now it seems, the work might simply be a pleasure whether housekeeping or study. Your kind words at the depot were so unexpected, so friendly, they gave and still give more help than you can guess, and I will thank you for them always."[4]

She did not have an easy time in Paris. The school attempted to delay releasing her diploma until she turned 30 and would no longer be eligible for graduation. Morgan countered by entering, anonymously, a competition given by the school and winning first prize, literally embarrassing the school into giving her the diploma she had earned. She finally returned to California in 1901 at the age of 29. She had planned to go to France for only two years at the most, and it was six years later when she returned home.

The winner of the Phoebe Apperson Hearst Competition for the University of California Campus was Émile Bénard, a Frenchman who had prepared his plan without seeing the site. To accommodate the plan to actual conditions, Bénard came to Berkeley and completed his revisions in 1900. He was offered the post of supervising architect, declined the job, and returned to Paris. In 1902, the job was offered to John Galen Howard, an elegant New Yorker who had attended MIT and the Beaux-Arts and who was serving on the Board of Advisors overseeing the realization of the plan. He was also asked to found a school of architecture and was offered the commission to design and build the Hearst Mining Building, which Phoebe Hearst donated to the university as a memorial to her husband, as well as the Greek Theater, which she had convinced her son, now almost 40, to donate to the university. Julia Morgan went to work with Howard and for two years worked on the Hearst projects.

At Phoebe Hearst's urging, in 1904, Morgan left Howard and opened her own architectural office, the first woman in California to be so licensed. In order to make development of Mills College for Girls a reality, Phoebe Hearst had commissioned Maybeck to design the overall campus plan. It is highly likely that she also convinced Mrs. Frank Marion Smith, who donated funds for a bell tower, to select Julia Morgan that same year as the architect for the structure, a substantial commission with which to launch an office. Morgan went on to design a library (1906), gymnasium (1908), and social hall (1916) for the college.

The patronage of Phoebe Hearst, with her influence in the Bay Area, coupled with Morgan's Beaux-Arts diploma convinced others to seek out her services in spite of her minimal experience, her age, and, most importantly, her sex. She would go on to design, it is estimated, almost 800 buildings of all types: YWCAs around the world, schools, the facilities at Asilomar, churches, hospitals, and private residences that rank among the best designed on the West Coast.

In 1892, Will Hearst had taken his first crack at building. He had long admired a 500-acre ranch near Pleasanton, south of Oakland, which his father had bought years before, and decided to enlarge the existing ranch house into a hunting lodge where he could entertain friends. He hired Bay Area architect A. C. Schweinfurth to design the project, and together they proceeded with extensive remodeling while tentatively discussing the possibility of a larger, grander structure. Hearst had forgotten, however, that the ranch was not his property; it was his mother's. Word of his enterprise reached her in Washington and she decided to return, not only to deal with her son's impulsiveness, but also to truncate his liaison with a certain Tessie Powers who, on and off, had been his mistress since his Harvard days.

The relationship was severed, but the hunting lodge was built. One of the first commissions Phoebe Hearst gave to Julia Morgan, in 1902, was the remodeling of the hunting lodge into a home for herself. Morgan produced the large and lovely Hacienda del Pozo de Verona for Mrs. Hearst, who decorated the house with some of the

The Hacienda del Pozo de Verona, near Pleasanton, was one of the grandest estates in California. Hearst sold the estate after his mother's death; it later became the Castle-wood Country Club and, in 1969, was almost completely destroyed by fire. Courtesy The Bancroft Library, Berkeley.

Opposite above: The Music Room at the Hacienda. Opposite below: A room in the Hacienda, which was remodeled for Phoebe Apperson Hearst by Julia Morgan. Both photographs c.1910; courtesy California Historical Society, San Francisco.

objects in her collection, filling it with tapestries, statues, paintings, and antiques. The house contained a music room that could accommodate 250 people comfortably, a Spanish-style dining room with bronze grille-work doors that Phoebe Hearst had brought from Spain, and an Italian wellhead that Will Hearst had installed out on the patio. The home was a meandering, stuccoed, Spanish-Moorish affair with balconies and patios, arcades and towers. It was the first residential work that Morgan did for the Hearsts and one certainly heavy with intimations of things to come.

Morgan first met Hearst while she was supervising construction of the Pleasanton house. He was then living in New York, running the *Journal*, and would come west annually to visit with his mother.

The contrasts and similarities of the two were marked. Morgan was small and shy to the point of invisibility. Hearst was also shy, but he could be quite gregarious at times and brimming with a fine humor. She was extremely wary of publicity and cultivated anonymity as a way of life, giving only one paragraph-long interview in her entire life. Morgan almost successfully escaped ever being photographed and was extremely reluctant to allow her work to be featured in the architectural press. She avoided social gatherings as much as possible and shunned participation in professional groups, although she did finally join The American Institute of Architects in 1921.

Hearst, on the other hand, had never been known to shy away from publicity. He not only thrust himself into view, but inhabited the consciousness of the age. Nonetheless, both Hearst and Morgan shared a fierce intelligence and love of architecture as well as a mutual respect which was to mature over the years of their association to the point where Morgan, among a handful of associates, could command and keep his undivided attention. She was also one of the few people around him who could keep pace with his furious drive.

During the first dozen years her office was open, Julia Morgan had some 200 commissions, which, in spite of her advantage of having Phoebe Hearst as a patroness, is all the more remarkable for the prejudice she had to fight in the business world generally and in the profession of architecture in particular. Contractors and workmen, however, did come to respect her knowledge and demand for craftsmanship as well as the soft finality with which she closed discussions. Walter Steilberg, a longtime associate of Morgan, said of her, "Nothing bothered her—she was fearless. She had a strain of steel in her I have never found in any other human being."[5]

She favored man-tailored jackets, worn over silk blouses, because the pockets eliminated the need for her to carry a purse, making it possible for her to scramble up ladders and scaffolding, along ledges, to be everywhere at once. She was a formidable supervisor of construction on the job site, and she would work 12, 14, 16 hours a day, sometimes seven days a week, and expected of her staff the same dedication and single-mindedness. Dorothy Wormser Coblentz, one of the many women who worked for Morgan, recalls that "the pressure was terrible. She didn't realize that people had private lives . . . time meant nothing to her. She went out of her way to hire women, but expected them to emulate her."[6]

And yet, hers was one of the most prestigious offices in San Francisco. Young graduates, male and female, would often attempt to find employment with Morgan. She ran her office as an atelier, a school of real work where she taught the skills necessary for architecture. Because they had been so well trained by her, her employees were always sought after by other offices. Also, Morgan did not have a great hunger for money. Her employees always shared in the profits, an almost unheard-of practice at the time. She would take what was needed for the office overhead and her personal expenses and distribute the remainder among her employees. She saw herself as an anonymous figure in a collective group of people who created buildings. The medieval notion of the Master Builder was her model for the architect's role.

She had a passion for detail and for quality, no matter what the size of the commission, that made her something of a legend among architects, clients, and contractors. She expected excellence and gave excellence. Julia Morgan and William Randolph Hearst were well matched in the dedication to and love for their respective professions and in the understanding of them. If she ever objected to his brand of journalism, she never mentioned it to anybody, remarking only that she did especially respect Hearst's knowledge and understanding of history, art, and horticulture. They both had the same quality of mind, "the kind of a mind that could use up subjects so much more quickly than people with smaller minds and needed more materials to chew on."[7]

Julia Morgan's office in San Francisco, along with those of John Galen Howard, Willis Polk, Ernest Coxhead, and Bernard Maybeck in Berkeley, while satisfying clients of the time with traditional architecture, were also creating a new style of residential architecture in Northern California. It was being done unconsciously because the self-effacing Morgan, especially, would never have dreamed of setting out to do something so deliberately ego-heralding as that. It simply emerged through her work. It was to become a style of architecture compounded out of simple shingled or stuccoed volumes sheltered under deep gabled roofs that were effortlessly compatible with the landscape. These buildings married the indoors and outdoors with terraces, balconies, and patios in a manner that perfectly suited the lifestyle that was emerging in the Bay Area. The work was a precursor to what Lewis Mumford, speaking later of that style (the post–World War II Bay Region style), would refer to as the first designs to put California architecture aesthetically on the modern map.

But Julia Morgan did not limit her work to any single style. She was most solicitous of her clients' needs and was able to create environments that could house their desires as well as express her own aesthetic preferences. Julia would meet with her clients in her office library and together they might leaf through one of her many source books until they found a building in a particular style that seemed appropriate for the client. Then, rather than vigorously copying that style or building, she would begin improvising on it so that the completed building, while being stylistically consistent, would also be distinctively hers. Unpretentious but meticulous detailing, the use of exposed structure, classical ornamentation placed against a functional joint, and particular attention to plan relationships were all devices, elaborations on an initial theme and the client's needs, that stamped a house as having been designed by Julia Morgan. Her buildings, like herself, have about them a contained, quiet elegance, understated but singularly correct.

She had been imbued with a rational, logical approach to design at the Beaux-Arts and never wavered from the practical and commodious use of structure, space, and form. She rejected innovation for its own sake and chose instead to adapt traditional forms to a specific situation or modify them to meet her clients' needs. The style in which Hearst and Morgan would finally build Casa Grande developed after a number of design changes on paper. When they first started discussing design in 1919, Hearst was of the opinion that the so-called San Diego look was not what he wanted, he wanted something more Renaissance in style. However, as Morgan developed her drawings, Hearst eventually changed his mind and the San Diego look emerged. It was a further refinement and outgrowth of the only authentic regional architectural style developed up to that time in California, a New World Spanish baroque style originating in Spain, which had evolved first in colonial Mexico and later in California.

That style had been given its first important public manifestation in California at the Panama-California International Exposition held in San Diego in 1915—a manifestation resonant of its beginnings in the Old World. Bertram Goodhue of New York served as supervising and consulting architect to the exposition. Goodhue decided that the buildings and grounds should be architecturally unified and culturally appropriate to California. He chose as his general influence the Churrigueresque architecture of Mexico, a fanciful, convoluted elaboration of the Spanish baroque, named after the Spanish architect José Churriguera. When the exposition opened, its impact upon California and, to a lesser degree, the rest of the country was astounding. Both the public and the architectural profession were struck by the significance of the development of a uniquely regional style that had its roots in its own history. Morgan and Hearst were quite familiar with the exposition and its architecture when, four years later, they embarked on their long building project.

But the year 1919 was marked for them by more than the inception of the project at San Simeon. That year Julia Morgan suffered a double tragedy. Her mother, to whom she had always been close, suffered a stroke, and Phoebe Apperson Hearst died, succumbing to the epidemic of influenza that swept the globe after World War I. Phoebe Hearst had contracted the illness in New York and, after a while, recovered; to recuperate further, she returned home to Pleasanton where she suffered, instead, a relapse. Will Hearst and his wife hurried out to be with her. Phoebe Hearst lingered for two more weeks after the relapse and then, on April 13, California's most formidable woman died. It was a grievous loss for both Hearst and Morgan.

SAN SIMEON: THE ARCHITECTURE

 A WEEK OR TWO before Phoebe Hearst's death at the Hacienda near Pleasanton, William Randolph Hearst visited the office of Julia Morgan in San Francisco in order to discuss a building project for his property at San Simeon. Walter Steilberg, an employee in the Morgan office who would later design much of the structural concrete work at San Simeon, recalls that he had stayed late that afternoon at his work and heard Hearst talking in the library with Morgan. Steilberg remembers hearing Hearst's high-pitched voice: "'I would like to build something up on the hill at San Simeon. I get tired of going up there and camping in tents. I'm getting a little old for that. I'd like to get something that would be more comfortable. The other day I was in Los Angeles, prowling around second-hand book stores . . . and I came upon this stack of books called Bungalow Books. Among them I saw this one which has a picture—this isn't what I want, but it gives you an idea of my thought about the thing, keeping it simple—sort of a Jappo-Swisso bungalow.' He laughed at that and so did she."[8]

The hill that Will Hearst was referring to was an elongated knob at the top of Camp Hill on the Piedra Blanca ranch he had long held in fond regard. As a youth he had camped and picnicked there with his father and friends, and later Hearst and his wife and sons continued visiting the ranch whenever possible, staying in a complex of tents on the top of the 1,600-foot-high hill. The tents would be erected to

View of San Simeon from China Hill.

house guests, servants, supplies, and kitchen and toilet facilities. There were often as many as 50 people in that temporary village engaging in all manner of entertainments prepared for them by their host. He would have dances, organize superb picnics on nearby mountains or on the beach, and make amateur movies, writing the scenarios and casting his guests and ranch hands in comically appropriate roles.

It was immediately evident that the simple bungalow theme would not prevail, and it was only about a month after that initial meeting that Julia Morgan, her office, and Hearst, even richer because of his inheritance, were entertaining more elaborate notions on a far more ambitious scale.

As with her other clients, Morgan was solicitous of Hearst's desires, and it is quite probable that Hearst himself chose to build in the Spanish colonial style after reviewing Morgan's source books in her office library. The architecture of the Spanish settlers had been derived from centuries of response to the demands of climate, landscape, and available local materials. It is not surprising that their long-nurtured architectural forms fit so well into the climate and landscape of Northern Mexico and Southern California, which is so similar to large areas of Spain.

While all cultures have defined themselves with their architecture, not all have done it so consistently and with such emphasis as the Old World Spanish. As did all people, they freely borrowed ideas and building techniques from neighboring cultures. They also were the inheritors of Islamic attitudes and forms thrust upon them during centuries of Arab occupation. Spanish-Moorish architecture is instantly recognizable, utterly authentic, and characteristically clear, in the sense that it does not confuse.

The height of the Spanish world empire in the 17th and 18th centuries coincided with the evolution and prevalence of Spanish baroque architecture—an architecture of florid and magnificent excess. Those centuries were also the period of great Mexican building activity. The Spanish colonial style of Mexico is characterized by many elements that distinguish the Churrigueresque. The exterior wall surfaces are, as a rule, broad, flat, and unembellished. Decorative urges are particularized and isolated, focused mainly on doorways, windows, towers, and, to a lesser extent, balconies, roofs, cornices, and interior ceilings and fireplaces.

By concentrating the mass of decorative detail in one area of a plain wall, the Spanish were able to focus attention for maximum visual effect, using limited means. Door and window openings are one of the major visual events of any building type, making the transition from the outside to inside. The Churrigueresque style celebrates and

Opposite: View of Casa Grande from distant Reservoir Hill.

announces that event by surrounding those openings with highly sculptural details. With the exception of certain Gothic cathedrals, Spanish baroque doorways and windows (and, by extension, Mexican) of the late Renaissance, with their legacy of Islamic art, are unparalleled in architectural history.

The disposition of building and garden elements on the hill at San Simeon is derived from the European town in general and the Mediterranean town in particular. Most cities and towns built in countries near the Mediterranean contain at least one major public open space surrounded and faced by smaller buildings with a church or palace or sometimes a municipal building on one side. It was this basic scheme that Julia Morgan used for Hearst's hill. The large cathedral-like mass of the main house—Casa Grande—looms over a large open terrace which, in turn, is surrounded by the guest houses and further defined by the landscaping.

The scheme for the overall organization of the hilltop emerged quite rapidly after the first meeting and was not to change for the life of the project. The design of individual parts, however, was to go through many stages and alterations. The Main Building was always intended to dominate the hill and the composition of surrounding smaller houses and terraces.

The top of the hill, in plan, is roughly an elongated oval oriented east and west. The long north and south sides are straight, the west end circular, and the east end somewhat flattened. The Main Building occupies the bulk of the area just east of the center of the oval. That building, schematically, is a rectangle with one long side removed. In the middle and perpendicular to the remaining long side is a stem of equal length that points west toward the Pacific Ocean.

A line drawn east to west through the center of the stem would divide the oval site in half. To the south of that line and parallel to it is the South Terrace. Somewhat to the north of that terrace on the circular west end but still south of the center line is House A. All the other buildings and terraces on the site lie to the north of the line. House C, which faces west, and C Terrace are slightly to the north of the line. Continuing around the circular end toward the northeast are the Neptune Terrace and Neptune Pool. These fall between House C and House B, which, with the North Terrace, lies along the straight north edge of the site. To the rear of Casa Grande in the northeast quadrant of the site is the indoor swimming pool, or Roman Pool, and some large outbuildings, which, in Hearst's day, were workshops and garages.

The contours of the hill were reshaped into basically five levels. Casa Grande and rear courtyard, main Terrace, and main gardens form the highest part of the site. The four remaining levels step

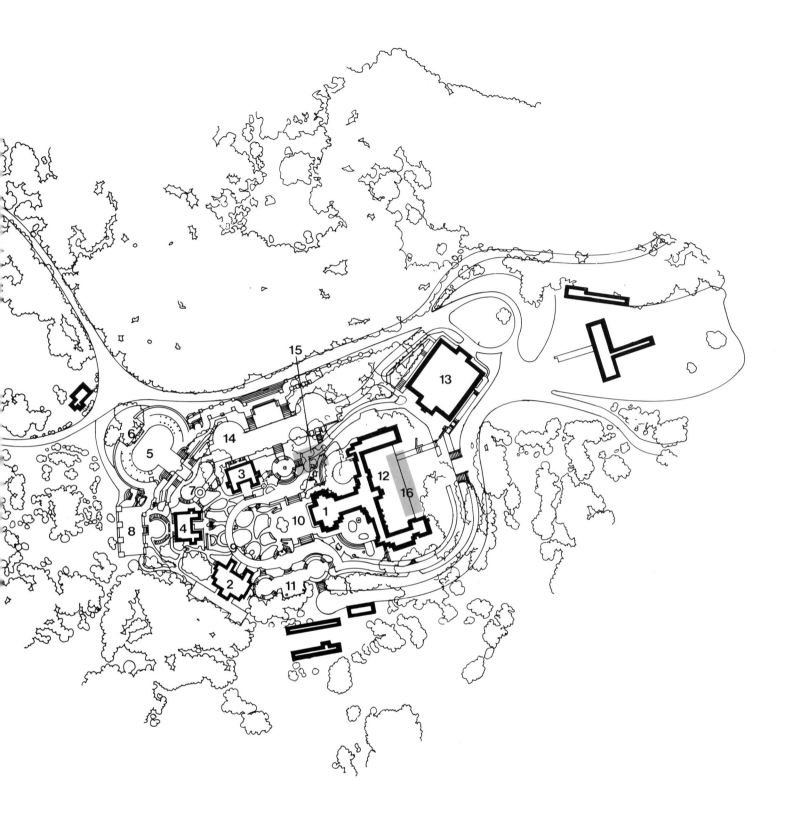

SITE PLAN OF SAN SIMEON

1	CASA GRANDE	**9**	ESPLANADE
2	CASA DEL MAR (A)	**10**	MAIN TERRACE
3	CASA DEL MONTE (B)	**11**	SOUTH TERRACE
4	CASA DEL SOL	**12**	REAR COURTYARD
5	NEPTUNE POOL	**13**	RECREATION BUILDING (INDOOR POOL)
6	TEMPLE FACADE	**14**	NORTH TERRACE
7	NEPTUNE TERRACE	**15**	SITE OF D HOUSE
8	C TERRACE	**16**	PROPOSED GREAT HALL

down and away on three sides: north, west, and south. The first level below Casa Grande and the Main Terrace is the Esplanade from which one enters the main floors of the three guest houses and part of their gardens. The floors of these houses and the adjacent gardens between them then step down along the contours of the hill and make the transition to the next lower level. This level is approximately the same as the lowest floors of the guest houses and contains the Neptune Terrace and the South Terrace.

Below the Neptune Terrace level is a walk which connects the area below House C with the western end of the North Terrace (unfinished), which is the largest of the formal terraces. Aligned east-west along the north edge of the site, this terrace was to have been part of a grand entrance stepping up the hill to the Main Terrace. The lowest formal level is that on which C Terrace and the Neptune Pool are built.

The gardens primarily occur between the level of the North Terrace and the Esplanade, and between the Esplanade and the Main Terrace. While the terraces and formal paths on the different levels are paved, most of the paths through the garden areas are unpaved, meandering, and informal, and establish an important contrast between the two kinds of experiences.

On an extended walk about the grounds, one is constantly aware of ascending and descending. The various levels are interconnected by numerous flights of formal and informal stairs. The three-dimensionality of the site is made astonishingly clear, both by the kinetic effort involved and by the continually shifting perspectives and changing spatial relationships of the buildings to each other. Not only were the buildings and grounds splendidly related horizontally, but the vertical relationships were handled equally well.

Julia Morgan drew upon two different but harmonious architectural styles to shape the buildings on the Enchanted Hill. The smaller houses were designed in what has been called the Mediterranean style, borrowed mainly from the Italian, and show much less of the Spanish influence of the Main Building. They recall the ambience and nuance of Italian villa architecture.

It had long been said by some that the inspiration for the towers of Casa Grande came from the tower of the cathedral in Ronda, Spain, perhaps by way of a source book in Julia Morgan's library. This point, however, had never been substantiated until, in a search for verification of another point in the California Historical Society archives, a misfiled postcard (part of a longer, undated letter) in Hearst's handwriting was found. This card once and for all authenticates the influence for the towers as Ronda. The card has a picture of the cathedral on one side and on the other side the message: "Now we have left Seville and are off to the country. This is the Cathedral

Above: The Cathedral of Santa Maria la Mayor in Ronda, Spain, was the inspiration for the design of Casa Grande's towers. Below: An early perspective study for Casa Grande showing incorporation of the Ronda tower motif. Opposite: Part cathedral, part mansion, Casa Grande assumes bold command of its hilltop setting.

Above: The south tower of Casa Grande from the Celestial Bridge. Opposite: Casa Grande's towers reflect the Spanish colonial spirit of the San Diego Panama-California International Exposition of 1915.

Left: View of the ocean from the Celestial Bridge between Casa Grande's towers. Above right: The Celestial Bridge and south tower. Below right: The top of the south tower with its 17th-century gilt-iron Venetian weather vane. Opposite: Detail of the south tower with ceramic tiles designed by Julia Morgan and a cast-stone panel of two angels flanking a portrait bust of a saint.

at Ronda. Do you recognize the tower? It is from this tower that Miss Morgan and I took the motif for the towers at the ranch. The Cathedral is a very quaint old building—very composite in style. In fact hardly in any style. It is attractive however. Ronda is. . . . " The letter is continued elsewhere, undiscovered; to whom it is addressed is also unknown.

For the exterior of Casa Grande, Morgan used as her primary influence the Spanish colonial or Churrigueresque, the elaborate style of Spanish baroque architecture, as recently translated by the New York architect Bertram Goodhue at the San Diego Panama-California International Exposition of 1915. Using carved and cast-stone detailing on the façade, she achieved an especially fine effect with the juxtaposition of the antique statuary and the new stonework around the front door. The shadows from the relief of the decoration make an easy transition from the blank, flanking light walls to the dark void of the doorway. The decorative elements focus attention on the entrance and further fuse the bottom half of the façade into a unified piece that is refreshingly innovative, immediately commanding interest, yet true to the stylistic spirit from which it springs.

The balconies and window frames, both new ones and those from Hearst's collection, were also handled in the Churrigueresque manner, as visual punctuation marks, something which the eye can rest upon and examine as it travels along the broad reaches of bare wall. In fact, all of the decorative elements on Casa Grande (and the other houses, in a more subdued way) are used in the characteristic Spanish colonial manner, even if the particular elements did not originate in Mexico or Spain or try to recall them. It was the way they were used so successfully by Morgan as punctuation, accent, and transitional devices that is important.

Although the planning and shipment of materials began in 1919, almost immediately after the meeting described by Steilberg, the actual construction at San Simeon began in 1920, and was to continue seamlessly until 1937. It was a project that would tax the ingenuity of everybody involved and the fortune of Hearst and his various corporations.

The main entrance in the lower half of Casa Grande's west elevation is an elaborate blend of contemporary limestone and cast-stone work with historical details such as the Gothic "wild men" at either side of the doorway, an equestrian figure immediately above, and, above that, under a canopy, a Madonna and Child. The large wrought-iron door combines 16th-century Spanish and contemporary craftsmanship.

Top left: A 13th-century Madonna and Child from northern Spain, installed under a Gothic-style canopy made in the 1920s, surmounts the main entrance of Casa Grande. Bottom left: "The Duke of Burgundy Going Hunting," a 15th-century limestone sculpture from France, immediately above the main entrance. Above: A pair of 16th-century Spanish portrait reliefs incorporated into the white limestone façade. Opposite left and right: A pair of "wild men" frame the doorway of Casa Grande much as they may have flanked a 15th-century Spanish cathedral's entry.

Detail of the front door of Casa Grande: a fanlight section made by Ed Trinkeller in the style of the 16th-century Spanish gate that it surmounts.

An ensemble of antique limestone columns and elaborately modeled cast-stone work forms the decorative surround for one of the Assembly Room's alcove windows. The wrought-iron grate with intricate cresting was made by Ed Trinkeller.

Italian Gothic window on the south façade of the new wing.

Window on the rear façade of Casa Grande.

Cast-stone reproduction on the new wing.

Italian Gothic window on the south façade of the new wing.

Balcony-window combination on the pantry.

Italian Gothic window on the south façade of the new wing.

Window on the rear façade of Casa Grande.

Window on the rear façade of Casa Grande.

Venetian triforium on the south façade of the new wing.

Italian Gothic window on the south façade of the new wing.

Italian Gothic window on the south façade of the new wing.

Italian Gothic window on the south façade of the new wing.

Italian Gothic window on the south façade of the new wing.

Window on the rear façade of Casa Grande.

Window on the Patio Vestibule.

Above: Display of antique windows on the new wing's south elevation.

Above: A pair of roof-line observers seem to look down upon the daring projection of a balcony.

Opposite
Above left: Casa Grande's central shank viewed from a back balcony of the Library. The upper reaches of the Refectory are marked by a row of Gothic-style windows; above them is the Cloister Gallery; the wood cornice on top forms the exterior of the Gothic Study. Below left: North end of a second-floor balustrade on the front façade: Saracen warriors armed with scimitars ride toward the center of the building. Right: Sharply cantilevered balconies on the second and third levels.

Construction was begun simultaneously on the three guest houses. House A, House B, and House C were so designated in order that Hearst and Morgan might keep track of which building they were referring to. Each house was also named for the major view seen from its living room window.

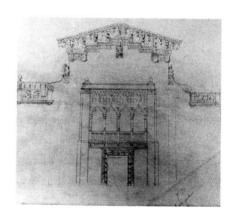

House A, Casa del Mar (House of the Sea), was the first building occupied on the site. The largest of the completed guest houses, it contains 14 rooms on two levels totalling 8,104 square feet. House B, Casa del Monte (House of the Mountain), started in 1920, is the smallest, with 10 rooms totalling 3,608 square feet. The last of the smaller houses to be completed was House C, Casa del Sol (House of the Sun), the most distinguished and architecturally elegant of the three. It contains 18 rooms but is smaller than House A, measuring 6,584 square feet on three levels that cascade down the hillside, surrounded by lovely gardens.

Below: Stone windows and balconies on the rear façade of Casa Grande. The square Doge's Suite loggia is 15th- or 16th-century Venetian. Two levels above, at the back of the third-floor Gothic Suite, is a set of windows from a 14th-century French church. Opposite above: An early freehand perspective for the rear of Casa Grande. The Doge's Suite loggia and the cornice are similar to what was actually built, but the entry from the rear courtyard has yet to be solved. Opposite below: Undated study by Julia Morgan (probably early 1920s) for the rear elevation of Casa Grande. The Doge's Suite loggia and the surmounting gable (later raised a level higher) look very much as they do today.

Opposite: View from the South Terrace with Casa del Mar in the background, below which the hill drops sharply to the coast. Above: Detail of the elaborately conceived cast-stone cornice of Casa del Mar. Below: An essentially Renaissance revival design prevails in Casa del Mar, the largest guest house. Courtesy California Historical Society, San Francisco.

Above: Bougainvillea frames the windows of Casa del Monte's back bedrooms. Left: A view from Casa Grande of Casa del Monte, the Esplanade, and the North Terrace, with the lower Big Sur country in the distance.

Overleaf
Left: A centuries-old live oak keeps the northwest corner of Casa del Monte in shade. Azaleas thrive underneath the great tree. Above right: Some of Ed Trinkeller's most intricate iron work is found in the doors at the rear courtyard of Casa del Monte. Below right: Formal symmetry and intimate scale distinguish the Italian Renaissance–style Casa del Monte.

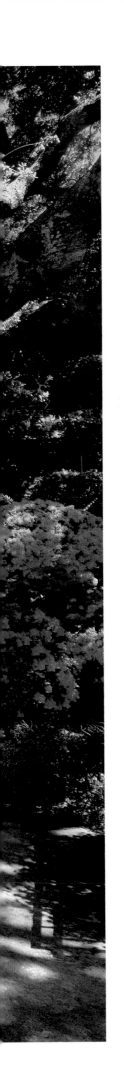

Above: Bougainvillea plants have nearly overtaken the lower walls of Casa del Sol's west side. A cast-stone Fu dog guards the lower entrance. Right: The spirit of Spanish colonial revival architecture is especially evident in Casa del Sol, with its Spanish-Moorish loggia and multiple roof lines. The lower court's limestone and marble fountain is more Italianate, as seen in this long view from C Terrace.

Right: "Adam and Eve," a bronze sculpture of 1925 by Arthur C. Walker in the court-yard west of Casa del Sol. Opposite: View of the square towers of Casa del Sol through a garden path. Art Deco sculptures in white Seravezza marble, by French sculptor Felix Fevola, decorate an intimate garden at the corner of the building.

Above and below left: Gilt lunette panels and part of a frieze of California-made tiles above the doors to Casa del Sol's east entry court. Top right: Detail of one of Casa del Sol's tile-decorated chimneys. Center and bottom right: Two of a group of 50 Persian tiles set around the east entry court doors.

72

Left: One of the numerous portrait heads in the two wrought-iron doors to Casa del Sol's east entry court by Ed Trinkeller. Below left: One of the east entry court's matching pair of wrought-iron doors. The tiny portrait heads are said to represent Trinkeller's fellow artisans. Below right: The lower suite of Casa del Sol is reached on the west side through a weblike wrought-iron door. Grilles of equally intricate design—one a Spanish original, the other a 1920s reproduction—cover the nearby windows. Tile and cast-stone details surrounding the door are contemporary.

In September 1926, Julia Morgan prepared schematic plans for House D. It was to have been the largest of all the guest houses, containing, on three levels, 15 bedrooms alone. It is not clear from the drawing where this house was to be sited. In the archives at San Simeon there are no site plans or further references made to House D at all, but, given the loosened formality of the site, the established axes, spatial thrusts and dispositions, there are only two sites that make any sense. The least convincing, if immediately obvious, site would be the area east of House A at the other end of the South Terrace. This location, however, would have closed the incredible and generous view of the coast. The more convincing location would have been east of House B at the end of the North Terrace, thereby framing what was to have been the main entrance to the complex. A formal set of stairs was to have climbed from the road to the center of the North Terrace and continued up to the Main Terrace in front of Casa Grande. The entrance stairs and processional spaces were never completed but the formality and visual distinction of that entrance would certainly have been made more powerful had it been symmetrically framed by two buildings. There are incomplete stair foundations that begin to climb the retaining wall and grade at that location on the North Terrace. The style of House D was to have been similar to that of the other guest houses.

Excavation for Casa Grande was also begun in 1920. The Main Building contains some 100 rooms including basements, vaults, and so on. There are 37 bedrooms, 12 of which are servants' rooms, 41 bathrooms, 14 sitting rooms, a hotel-size kitchen and pantry, plus

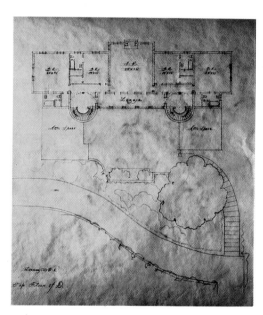

Plan for the top floor of the proposed House D, a three-level structure that was never built. The drawings date to 1926.

The unfinished grand entrance, between the driveway and the North Terrace, with its two flights of concrete steps now overgrown with ivy. Exposed ends of vertical reinforcing bars indicate where balustrades would have been attached.

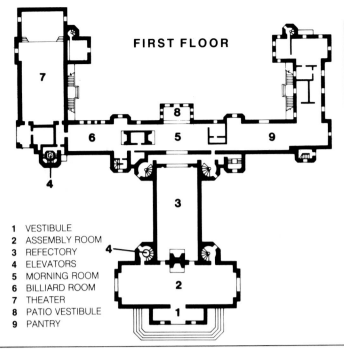

FIRST FLOOR

1 VESTIBULE
2 ASSEMBLY ROOM
3 REFECTORY
4 ELEVATORS
5 MORNING ROOM
6 BILLIARD ROOM
7 THEATER
8 PATIO VESTIBULE
9 PANTRY

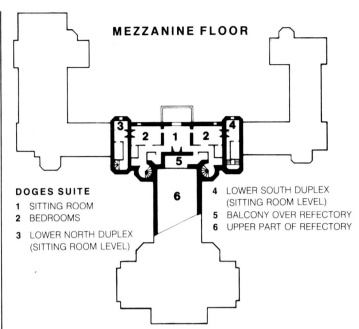

MEZZANINE FLOOR

DOGES SUITE
1 SITTING ROOM
2 BEDROOMS
3 LOWER NORTH DUPLEX
   (SITTING ROOM LEVEL)

4 LOWER SOUTH DUPLEX
   (SITTING ROOM LEVEL)
5 BALCONY OVER REFECTORY
6 UPPER PART OF REFECTORY

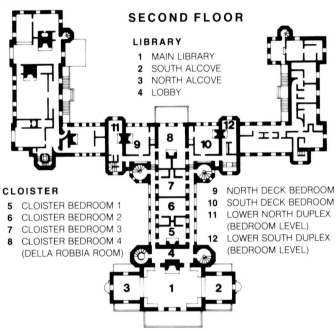

SECOND FLOOR

LIBRARY
1 MAIN LIBRARY
2 SOUTH ALCOVE
3 NORTH ALCOVE
4 LOBBY

CLOISTER
5 CLOISTER BEDROOM 1
6 CLOISTER BEDROOM 2
7 CLOISTER BEDROOM 3
8 CLOISTER BEDROOM 4
   (DELLA ROBBIA ROOM)

9 NORTH DECK BEDROOM
10 SOUTH DECK BEDROOM
11 LOWER NORTH DUPLEX
   (BEDROOM LEVEL)
12 LOWER SOUTH DUPLEX
   (BEDROOM LEVEL)

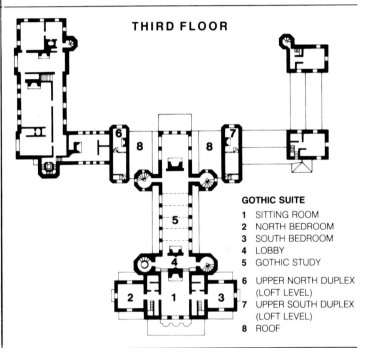

THIRD FLOOR

GOTHIC SUITE
1 SITTING ROOM
2 NORTH BEDROOM
3 SOUTH BEDROOM
4 LOBBY
5 GOTHIC STUDY
6 UPPER NORTH DUPLEX
   (LOFT LEVEL)
7 UPPER SOUTH DUPLEX
   (LOFT LEVEL)
8 ROOF

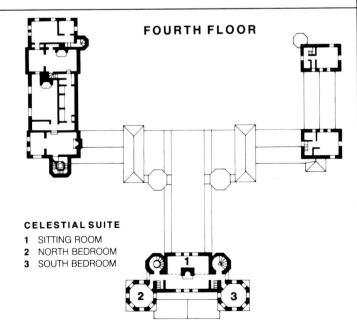

FOURTH FLOOR

CELESTIAL SUITE
1 SITTING ROOM
2 NORTH BEDROOM
3 SOUTH BEDROOM

FLOOR PLANS OF CASA GRANDE

the grand special rooms. It measures a total of 73,510 square feet, or almost one and a half times the size of a football field.

Casa Grande has about it two basic plan characteristics that distinguish it from other large residences built before or since. It also departs radically from some of the then prevailing notions governing large-scale residential design, and not for reasons of its size alone. The rooms and floors of the building are disposed not unlike those of a hotel, which is, after all, how the building functioned most of the time. The ground floor is given over to public rooms: lounges, recreational areas, dining room, and so on, with the sleeping facilities on the upper floors. This is not so different, in fact, from the disposition of rooms in any traditional two-story home. But one of the things that makes Casa Grande very different from a hotel or home of the period is that there is no apparent physical or spatial connection between the ground floor and those above.

Most hotels and residences have, in a visually prominent location, a flight of stairs connecting the lower floor with the one immediately above. The stair usually rises from a foyer and does three things for the viewer's perception. First, in a larger building such as a hotel or mansion, it acts as a focal point, a place of reference for those unfamiliar with the building. Second, it announces that there is another level above, where something is happening, and invites the viewer to participate, to ascend to that other floor. Third, it connects, spatially and visually, the different levels.

Casa Grande has no main stair or foyer. Each of the floors is visually, spatially, and experientially a separate entity. There is no sense, no clue at all, that anything is occurring above or below any of the floors. The only clear statement made is from the outside of the building, where it is apparent that there is more than one floor.

One has to learn how to move vertically through the building. The vertical connections—stairs and elevators—are hidden in stair towers that cannot be seen from any of the major rooms on the ground floor and are only incidentally glimpsed on the upper floors. They surely were not viewed as something to celebrate architecturally; instead, they have about them the strict functional necessity of a toilet.

The locations of the stairs can cause a great deal of confusion to the uninitiated, since a stair used in the morning might not be the stair used at night, placing the user in a wholly different relationship with his or her destination. Excluding the upper floors of the new wing (which were never used), there are six stair towers in the public part of the Main Building and only after some time does the user become familiar enough with the circulation patterns to avoid disorientation.

This hermetic and episodic spatial experience occurs horizontally as well as vertically, especially on the ground floor. Movement along

Opposite: Casa Grande's Main Vestibule contains two of the estate's most impressive architectural features: a 40-foot-long mosaic pavement of Roman origin and a marble doorway attributed to Andrea Sansovino, a 16th-century Florentine sculptor. Through the entry to the Assembly Room can be seen the Great Barney Mantel, a 16-foot-high French Renaissance fireplace surmounted by a pair of marble busts by François Duquesnoy. The Barney Mantel, named for turn-of-the-century tycoon Charles T. Barney in whose New York residence it had been installed, is one of the Assembly Room's dominating features. Above it hangs a silver- and gold-embroidered Italian velvet panel from the New York collection of William Salomon; on the table is a 16th-century rock crystal casket that was given to Hearst by French and Company in 1927; flanking the casket are two bronzes from the collection of Thomas Fortune Ryan.

that floor is not easily processional. That is, the rooms are, to a very large degree, separated from one another both physically and thematically. Each room is a complete visual experience in itself, having no sense of spatial participation with adjacent rooms. One is completely in the Assembly Room and then abruptly passes completely into the Refectory, and so on. Thus the experience of the place is serial and episodic with little or no transitional space occurring between one thematically decorative room and the next.

In order to move from one end of the ground floor to the other—say, from the Assembly Room to the Theater, which was the path of the evening's events—it is necessary to go through each of the rooms serially: Assembly Room, Refectory, Morning Room, and Billiard Room. There is no corridor, no alternate route other than by going outside or upstairs and down. While this is not entirely unique in European palatial design—Versailles comes to mind—it is certainly strange in the context of residential design in the United States.

On the second floor, the Library and the bedroom suites known collectively as the Cloisters are accessible by corridors and while the circulation is not crystal clear, it does have a readily learned logic. Furthermore, nostalgic about his early days on the hill, Hearst had Morgan model the basic scheme for the other bedroom suites here (except for the duplexes) and in the guest houses on the tents in which he, his family, and guests had stayed while camping. The large, rectangular World War I surplus Army tents were arranged with bedrooms at either end of a sitting room.[9] Entrance to the tents was by a doorway to the sitting room. If this scheme was simple, it was also practical, and contributed at times to interesting socializing.

Between the first and second floors, over the Morning Room, taking advantage of the space made available by the double-height Assembly Room and Refectory, at the rear of the building are the Doge's Suite and two of four small duplex suites on either side. Above the Doge's Suite, on the second floor, is the Della Robbia Room, several steps higher than the Cloisters. The second two duplex

Opposite: The palpable atmosphere common to all of San Simeon's rooms when lit at night is perhaps at its best in the gigantic Assembly Room with its soft electric lights suspended from a monumental Italian Renaissance ceiling. Among the riches to be seen in this room are the 17th-century "Triumph of Religion" tapestry, made in Brussels from a design by Peter Paul Rubens, which hangs in the north alcove, and the four large "Scipio Africanus" tapestries, designed by Giulio Romano, an Italian of the 16th century, which hang on the two long walls. At each side of the "Rubens" tapestry is a Carrara marble medallion by the Danish sculptor Albert Bertel Thorvaldsen.

Opposite: The ultra-Gothic Refectory seems to embody the essence of Hearst's magnificent taste. Silver gleams against a backdrop of 16th-century Gothic tapestries and 15th-century Spanish choir stalls. Below the coffered Italian ceiling hang bright banners of the districts of Siena. At the far end of the room a fragment of a French Gothic cloister forms a balcony loft, sometimes used for entertainment during dinner.

Below: Somber, medieval opulence characterizes the Morning Room at the back of Casa Grande. One of the room's three sanctuary lamps of hammered silver hangs from a rugged Spanish-Moorish ceiling in this view. On the walls can be seen a 17th-century Flemish tapestry and a 15th-century tempera-on-panel triptych from Aragon, Spain; in the foreground are two 18th-century Spanish armchairs from a Mexican convent. The Verona marble floor is a stylish departure from the travertine found in most parts of the building.

Above: The motif for the Theater's huge caryatids was derived from a much smaller 17th-century Spanish figure.

Left: Between the Morning Room and the Theater is the Billiard Room, essentially medieval in character but with an Oriental accent of 16th- to 18th-century Persian tile panels and spandrels. A 15th-century northern Spanish ceiling, a millefleur "hunting" tapestry, 18th-century gilt-wood chandeliers, and 1920s game tables make for an ingenious blend of old and new.

The nearly 90-foot-long Library on the second floor is an architectural treasure house of Spanish-Moorish ceiling work and a showcase for an important collection of ancient Greek vases, the majority of which are displayed on the plate rail above the contemporary walnut bookcases. The largest of Casa Grande's Italian mantelpieces—a limestone example attributed to the sculptor and architect Benedetto da Maiano—is set in the middle of the long side of the room. On the Italian table in the foreground is a finely sculpted Parian marble Roman vase.

Overleaf
Left: Hearst's private Gothic Study takes up the back half of Casa Grande's third floor. The murals on the arches were painted by San Simeon craftsman Camille Solon. Among the numerous works of art in the room is a large 16th-century Flemish dinanderie candlestick on the drop-leaf table in the foreground. Very fine objects in brass, ivory, and silver gilt fill the cases underneath the bookshelves. Above right: The most sumptuous of the guest rooms in Casa Grande is the Doge's Suite, located on the first floor's mezzanine level over the Morning Room. In the north bedroom a superb silver-and gold-embroidered altar frontal from the Phoebe Hearst collection hangs above the 17th-century bed. Below right: In the south bedroom of the Doge's Suite, behind the Florentine gilt-wood bed, is a Netherlandish cope of gold-embroidered velvet, c. 1500; the rectangular hanging is a 17th-century Italian table cover with its entire field richly decorated in needlework.

Each of the four duplex suites at the back of Casa Grande is a self-contained apartment with a small sleeping loft tucked above the first-level bathroom, leaving the sitting area open to a high and elaborately decorated ceiling. Lavish gold-leaf ornament is very effectively played against plain stucco surfaces in these unusual rooms of the 1930s. In the Lower South Duplex, shown here, two canvases by the French painter Simon Vouet (1590–1649) are incorporated into the contemporary ceiling.

A little-known room of grace and charm is the Lower North Duplex. Part of the interior of a Spanish building—the so-called Granada House—has been installed here in the form of columns, railings, and related elements. Below the balconied sleeping loft is a 13-light iron candelabrum from Spain; to its right, a tiny teak staircase ascends to the loft. This and similar staircases for the three other duplexes were produced by master woodcarver Jules Suppo in the 1930s.

suites, comprised by the upper half of the second floor and the lower half of the third floor, are not connected horizontally with the third floor, which contains Hearst's private Gothic Study and Gothic Suite. And above that suite, in the towers and the room that joins them, is the famous Celestial Suite.

Why Morgan and Hearst arrived at such an overall scheme, with its lack of reference space or visible stairs and its serially episodic room arrangements, is not known. One reason might be in the fact that the plan of the ground floor of the central portion of the building clearly resembles the plan of an early Christian basilica. The Morning Room, flanked by the pantry and Billiard Room, would be the narthex of the church, the Refectory the nave without side aisles, the Assembly Room the transept, and the Main Vestibule the apse; except, of course, that the sequence occurs in reverse order to that of a church since the main façade and entrance at San Simeon is where the apse, or rear, of a church would be.

If one follows the sequence of these axially aligned rooms from the rear courtyard, east to west (the same orientation as in early Christian churches), to the Assembly Room and entrance, it is evident that the rooms get increasingly larger and that the quality of the art and decoration becomes more important and the rooms themselves more carefully considered, more carefully designed. An entrance sequence proceeding from the courtyard would have allowed the viewer's experience to culminate in the Assembly Room, surely a grander visual experience than the one that occurs in which scale and grandeur diminish as one proceeds from the entry.

If it was their intention, after all, to work within the contours of and imply the form of a church, then that might explain the lack of a major foyer and stair engaging the lower and upper floors, as churches do not contain stairs within the body of their great spaces. Also, a church is usually a single unified space and not suitable for living unless separated into rooms. But here the rooms are not only separated from one another owing to functional necessity; they are divorced from one another to an extent that violates the spatial consequences of what might have been the intent of the plan. This is not to diminish the result, but it, with the reverse sequence of the hermetic spaces, does render the result contradictory as well as curious.

Opposite above: Exposed concrete framing and gleaming monel metal surfaces in Casa Grande's pantry typify the straightforward institutional approach to the service wing. Opposite below: Art Deco brass faucet handles and tulip-motif tiles from the Netherlands are among the few decorative elements in the otherwise spare pantry.

Above: Detail of a gilt and polychromed, craftsman-made plaster of Paris ceiling in Casa del Sol. Below: Detail of glazed ceramic tiles and plain terra-cotta pavers in the floor of Casa del Sol's main sitting room.

The ornate lower lobby of Casa del Mar is rich in gilt-decorated plaster of Paris ceilings, pilasters, and doorways. Of special interest among the works of art here are the polychromed stucco relief of the Madonna and Child by Mino da Fiesole, a 15th-century Florentine sculptor, and the gilt-wood, marble-topped 18th-century table from Italy.

The smaller houses, on the other hand, are all quite clear and straightforward in plan and function. They were just sleeping facilities, albeit sumptuous and well crafted. They contain only bedrooms and bathrooms flanking common sitting rooms and were not provided with any kitchens or recreational rooms. While the interiors are handsomely decorated and the exteriors graciously proportioned, they were conceived as participating with and being more a part of the gardens—providing a context for Casa Grande—than as significant pieces of architecture in themselves. These houses are beautiful examples of Italianate villa design, but their individual architectural significance is mitigated by the role that they play in creating a context for the Main Building. Skillfully married to the terraces, they form a partially enclosing wall—a plane—which, from the central terrace in front of Casa Grande, partially defines that outdoor space. From afar the guest houses visually are part of the terraces, gardens, and walls that step back and up, shaping the manmade top of the hill and providing a generous base for Casa Grande.

Left: One of Casa del Mar's larger second-floor bedrooms contains a 16th-century Spanish bed that was copied by Julia Morgan's craftsmen in order to provide a matching pair for the room (the nearer bed is the original). Below: In the second-floor sitting room of Casa del Mar are 16th-century wall hangings of Genoese velvet combined with gilt-plaster decoration, producing an extremely lavish effect.

Overleaf

Left above: The sitting room in Casa del Monte has a 1920s ceiling, a 15th- or 16th-century Renaissance mantelpiece supporting a bust of Philip II of Spain, and, along its east wall, two exceptionally fine examples of French Renaissance cabinetwork between which hangs a mid-19th-century painting by a Mexican artist, Juan de Lara. Left below: This immense velvet-canopied bed of rather mysterious lineage was originally used by William Randolph Hearst in his Casa del Mar suite. It was later moved to a room in Casa del Monte where this photograph was made (although it has recently been returned to its original location). The bedposts are carved and gilt columns large enough to have been at one time architectural components of a building, probably in Spain. Right: Probably no object at San Simeon has been publicized as much as Casa del Monte's Cardinal Richelieu Bed, whose name, it turns out, has no basis in historical fact. How the bed came by its fanciful sobriquet is uncertain; the coat of arms in the massive headboard is that of the Boffa family of Lombardy; the miter that surmounts the headboard suggests that this unique specimen of 17th-century furniture was made for a bishop. Behind the bed hangs a Flemish tapestry with the arms of a cardinal archbishop as the dominating motif. The elaborate Spanish-inspired gilt-plaster ceiling contains 24 faces, said to represent the hours of the day.

The upper section of Casa Grande under construction. In the foreground can be seen a completed section of the Esplanade. Photograph c. 1925.

Building on Camp Hill, as it was known in George Hearst's day, or La Cuesta Encantada, as Hearst sentimentally renamed it, was not anywhere near a normal construction project. Halfway between San Francisco and Los Angeles, along an isolated coast, it was essentially inaccessible by road and some 40 miles from the nearest railway. All building supplies except water, but including the aggregate for the concrete and the topsoil for the gardens, were brought in by coastal steamer, an overnight trip from San Francisco. The supplies would be unloaded on the pier that Hearst had rebuilt down in the village of San Simeon and then hauled by truck, and sometimes by cart, up the winding, treacherous, six-mile road from beach to summit. Because of that road and the nature of the job, most of the workers had to live on the site. During the 1930s it was the largest private construction job in California, employing hundreds of San Luis Obispo County residents in the midst of the Great Depression.

With so much construction going on, keeping the workers busy usually was not difficult but was extremely complicated. The logistics of material deliveries, schedule of priorities for various tasks, and ordered sequence of construction had to be carefully orchestrated. If a portion of the construction was occasionally disrupted because of a kink in the supply chain, it meant that a particular craft would have to be idled. If that craft—say carpentry—was idled, then every craft that followed the carpenters would also be idled in turn unless shifts to other parts of the project could be improvised. There had to be a certain amount of continuous building going on in order to maintain on the site a minimum complement of crew with all the necessary

skills. The work force for years averaged about 80 or 90 men, going sometimes as low as 25 and as high as 125, depending on desired activity, money available, and supplies on hand.

By 1922, work was proceeding on every part of the hilltop, though it did not progress continuously or simultaneously; even Hearst did not have that much money. During the winter, outdoor work would usually cease and indoor work would proceed at a quickened pace. Given the average number of workmen available, Morgan would have to move them about to satisfy priorities or whatever special conditions arose. Thus, while the Roman Pool took five years to finish, it was not worked on without interruption during those five years.

The Main Building, smaller houses, both pools, terraces, and retaining walls were built of reinforced concrete. The concrete was mixed on the site and was placed without the assistance of those devices such as pumps and conveyor belts that are so common today. Laborers pushed wheelbarrow loads of concrete along scaffolding to where it had to be dumped around steel reinforcing rods between form boards. The structural systems of all the buildings are generally similar. In Casa Grande, concrete trusses span from the outside structural walls; the trusses carry the weight of the concrete floor slabs and floor loads above them as well as the decorative ceilings hung from those trusses and from slabs on metal rods.

The ordering of supplies, making up of schedules and manpower assignments, direction of all the simultaneous bits and pieces of the project, as well as the disbursement of payments—the entire con-

View from the site of the Neptune Pool of all the buildings under construction: Casa del Monte to the left, Casa Grande's towers behind native California bay trees, and Casa del Sol with Casa del Mar to the right and behind it. Photograph c. 1925.

struction management, as it were—were under the charge of Julia Morgan and her office. She was assisted by a superintendent and architect on the site and by a bookkeeping staff in her office.

The design and building of the complex was not only beset by problems of isolation and material delivery, it was also occasionally inhibited and made more difficult by Hearst's personal quirks. Many people have said he could be arrogant and willful with people in order to achieve his desires. Walter Steilberg tells of an incident that speaks to what many perceived as Hearst's cavalier disregard of costs and, more importantly, of craftsmen's feelings: "I was there [in House C]. The fireplace had been located on the long side of one of the living rooms. He came in, and...said, 'No, I don't like it there. Take it out and move it over here.'" It was, Steilberg goes on, "all built! Chimney going clear up to the roof, and everything, and the foundation went to hell and gone down the hillside. I was also there when, six months later, Hearst said, 'No, that was a mistake. We shouldn't have moved it from where it was.'"[10] Hearst then ordered the fireplace rebuilt in its original location.

According to Steilberg, this sort of thing occurred frequently, out of a kind of childish willfulness. He also says that more than one craftsman stormed off the hill in spite of the good wages received. Morgan, who was also a victim of that sort of fickleness, once commented that the work on the hill entailed as much demolition of completed work as construction of new work. That, however, could have been the result of her wanting a change as well as Hearst, since she was also a perfectionist.

All three smaller houses were substantially complete when Hearst, his wife, five sons, and guests arrived on July 3, 1921, to occupy the buildings for the first time. The site of Casa Grande was a chaos of construction, and, perhaps for this reason, the boys stayed that summer in the ranch houses near the village of San Simeon. Hearst, then 58 years old, had embarked on a project that would be taxing enough for any one person's entire life, and he did it while running his publishing empire and his movie studio, collecting art objects, remaining politically active, and seeing to the rest of his affairs, which included other building projects as well. Among the various construction projects he engaged in were a huge 110-room beach house in Santa Monica for Marion Davies, furnished from his collection; St. Donat's in Wales, an 800-year-old castle set on 13,000 acres of land, which he purchased for $120,000 in 1925 and on which he spent a fortune, remodeling its 135 rooms; Wyntoon, the old family estate on the McCloud River in Northern California, which he rebuilt and substantially expanded; and the Long Island estate of Mrs. O. H. P. Belmont, purchased for $400,000 in 1927 for his wife Millicent. A 1935 *Fortune* magazine article on the Hearst organization estimated that he had spent close to $20,000,000 on all of his various construction projects.

Hearst, as profligate as he was with money, was extremely slow in paying bills either for art works acquired or for work or supplies that Morgan had authorized with his approval. Creditors would descend on her, pleading, threatening, distracting her from her work, upsetting schedules, and frustrating her financial projections. She sent Hearst a memo of succession a couple of times, a clear statement of what steps should be taken to replace her with another architect so that she could withdraw from the scene for awhile. She eventually stabilized the situation, finally getting Hearst to agree that he would have sufficient funds deposited in a bank for her to draw upon monthly after an agreed upon amount of work had been completed. So the work went on, three steps forward, one backward. A new fireplace purchased that must be installed, hardware in all the guest houses changed, the completed towers on Casa Grande must be raised so that the Celestial Suite could be added (it was finished and furnished in 1932). Big things and small things. Hearst built as though he were drawing in charcoal: the whole image would eventually emerge, but there would be erasures and corrections along the way.

These must have been seen as small irritants by Morgan when viewed against the scale of the project, and the relationship that these two remarkable people had established. At dinner in the Refectory the slight, plain Morgan, surrounded by the glitter and glibness of Hollywood, the studied pandering of politicians, and those truly talented—Charlie Chaplin, Bill Tilden, Dorothy Parker, and others of international fame—was one of the few guests who could command and hold Hearst's full attention. Seated opposite each other, they would discuss and review work, consider design changes, pass drawings back and forth, and would note here and jot there. They would remain seemingly oblivious of the rest of the guests until Morgan had finished discussing with Hearst that which she had intended to discuss and until Hearst had finished responding.

During the first hectic decade of construction, Morgan would come down from San Francisco weekly to supervise the work for quality and to confer with Hearst. Later the visits would occur with less frequency. On the average, though, as long as construction was actively pursued, she probably visited San Simeon every two weeks. She would usually take the train, the "Owl," leaving San Francisco at 8:00 P.M. Since she was unable to sit up in a lower berth, she would book an upper and usually work the entire trip at her portable drafting board as the train rumbled south to San Luis Obispo. Arriving about 2:00 A.M., she would snack on a bowl of milk and bread before continuing either in one of Hearst's cars or in a taxi, driving for hours over dirt roads the 40 miles from San Luis Obispo to San Simeon. She would usually be away from her office for a day and two nights, but occasionally she would stay longer.

Upon arriving, she would spend much time with her client in the shack in the courtyard that was her office or walking about on the terraces in intense discussions. Hearst's indispensable secretary, Joe Willicombe, known as the Colonel, would sometimes accompany them, keeping written track of the flurry of decisions they made. She would then confer with the superintendent of construction, for the first eight years of the project Herbert Washburn, and then Camille Rossi, a flamboyant character given to fighting bulls on vacations in Mexico, who was superintendent until the early 1930s.

These were the men in charge of the site. They oversaw the day-by-day detailed construction and were instruments of Morgan's authority. She would clamber about the construction scaffolding and examine the placing and quality of the concrete or the installation of a ceiling or some panelling and then closet herself again with Hearst to discuss further the proportion of a door or perhaps the location of a statue.

She worked in the wood shack in the courtyard of the Main Building when she was at the hill, and when she was not there resident draftsmen occupied it. The pace she kept on the hill was as furious as was her pace elsewhere, and while there she supposedly never took part in any of the social activities on the hill other than dinner.

During the week and at those times when Hearst was away from San Simeon, they would correspond endlessly by letter or telegram. The correspondence is direct, always to the point, and often filled with a sly humor. They would discuss various issues, from the grounds and buildings to the morale of the workers. They would arrive at conclusions and the work would proceed; whether the decision or work remained final was another matter.

February 21, 1927 [letter]

Dear Miss Morgan:

Please do not think I am altogether mad, but Mr. Swinnerton suggests something which may be worth while considering. On the other hand it may not be possible or desirable.

He suggests that between the towers on the third floor of the north wing we have a studio for artists.

We would have a wonderful north light and ample space for the kind of thing that an artist wants.

If we cannot put the studio here we ought to try to work it in somewhere, because we will have artists here in the future as we have had them in the past. . . .

Sincerely[11]

The south, or service, wing, which comfortably housed 20 to 25 servants. The small wood structure with a sloping roof was the "job shack" that Julia Morgan and her construction superintendent used throughout the 1920s and '30s.

February 25, 1927 [letter]

Dear Mr. Hearst:

To add to the studio on the north wing would be virtually the addition of a third story. Would it not unbalance the Patio? A third story on the south also, would bring the roof line so high the eaves would be practically on a line with those of the Main Building.

Could the studio be housed in the Chinese Hill group or possibly the Tennis Court development?

Yours very truly,
Julia Morgan[12]

Unfortunately the addition mentioned above did eventually occur, and the grace and proportions of Casa Grande suffered somewhat for it.

April 24, 1927 [telegram]

Julia Morgan, Merchants Exchange, San Francisco, Calif.
Suggest travertine for Gothic suite bedrooms and sitting rooms and possibly also for tower rooms if this meets with your ideas. 2. Please install all electric heater units as originally planned. They will be very valuable for chilly evenings when it is not desirable to keep steam heat going. 3. Building proper work must certainly take precedence over roads, fences, etc. There is no great hurry about roads and no hurry at all about fences.

W. R. Hearst[13]

June 3, 1927 [letter]

Dear Mr. Hearst:

. . . The Gothic Sitting Room ceiling is in and Gyorgy is finishing it. It took some real good nature on the part of the "wormers" to match up new with old work. The other two ceilings are up and Gyorgy's work on them well along.

Yours very truly,
Julia Morgan[14]

July 27, 1927 [letter]

Dear Mr. Hearst:

. . . Am I to plan on another month large allowance? We have put the labor before the material for the past two months and have to meet steel, marble, stone, plumbing and other material bills the first of the month. It is so easy this weather to run far ahead of the budget. . . .

Yours very truly
Julia Morgan[15]

The letters and telegrams flowed constantly between them, discussing in detail, details. Sash locks to be changed, drafts to be defeated, mantels to be used, the color of draperies and flowers. It was, along with everything else, a mighty task just to keep up with the correspondence.

According to the account of Morgan North, Julia Morgan's nephew, recollected years later, the architect was not particularly proud of the building. She continued with it because, "Well, ... if someone else had done it, ... it would have been worse."[16]

There was obviously more to it than that. There was the utter challenge of it all, the construction challenge which she always loved and the challenge of putting together such a puzzle from so many different pieces. She understood that Hearst was living in a totally unique, almost unreal world, a world in which he could buy anything he wanted, yet Morgan respected him perhaps more than any other person she worked with. She was simply not interested in his personal life, his politics, or how he made his money. He was someone with whom she could speak about art and architecture, who shared her enthusiasm for construction, and had given her an incredible opportunity. She was designing and building something that was improbable enough to build during the booming 1920s let alone during the Depression. Morgan had the opportunity to practice architecture in the boldest possible manner, calling on all of her training and practical experience. It was the chance of a lifetime and she surely knew it for that.

She knew, also, that she was building not only for Hearst but for the future. Building at the ranch also offered her a chance to realize a hope she had long held for architectural museums. "Of course," she said to Walter Steilberg, "this is just temporary—for his use. The country needs architectural museums, not just places where you hang paintings and sculptures."[17]

In that dream Hearst concurred. He knew he was only a temporary inhabitant of the place, and later, in his will, he would express the desire that the University of California take it over, and, as early as 1927, he was speaking of it as a museum.

February 19, 1927 [letter to Morgan]

... A great many very fine things will be arriving for the ranch—some of them had already arrived.

They are for the most part of a much higher grade than we have had heretofore. In fact, I have decided to buy only the finest things for the ranch from now on, and we will probably weed out some of our less desirable articles.

I had no idea when we began to build the ranch that I would be here so much or that the construction itself would be so important. Under the present circumstances, I see no reason why the ranch should not be a museum of the best things that I can secure....

Sincerely[18]

He entertained the idea of weeding out the less desirable pieces but did not carry it out. He improved the place by adding more good articles, but he let most of the pre-1927 items remain.

One project, an addition to Casa Grande, for which he and Morgan had great enthusiasm, indicates their ambitiousness and the degree to which they were willing to entertain improvisations. In a letter to Julia Morgan, written in 1932, he describes "a great ballroom and banqueting hall." The room would have been 150 feet long and was to have joined the service wing on the south with the theater wing (new wing) on the north, enclosing the east courtyard, which can be seen from his study. He had planned to hang eight great Gothic tapestries, each about 26 by 14 feet, four on each side of the room, and he also planned to have a 50-foot-wide central entrance under a rotunda on axis with the Main Building. At each end of the room, he wrote Morgan, he would place some "French flamboyant Gothic fireplaces" he had buried in his Bronx warehouses. As originally described, the room was to be 40 feet wide and at least as high as the Refectory. "When this hall is not in use as a ballroom or a banqueting hall, it could be used to contain some of the important collections in cases in the middle of the room. We could also use a lot of armor there."[19]

He thought it would be the crowning glory of the hilltop and planned to install a Spanish ceiling 103 feet long by 20 feet wide. "That is the scheme!" he went on, "Isn't it a pippin?" Hearst gleefully signed, "Sincerely, Your Assistant Architect."[20] Morgan, who was equally enthusiastic about the project, agreed with uncharacteristic excitement in a telegram to Hearst that, yes, "It certainly will be a marvelous room, as you say, a pippin."[21]

They discussed and designed the project by letter, telegram, no doubt by phone, and certainly in person when she brought a model of it down to San Simeon. They fueled each other's eagerness throughout that year, yet they finally dropped it, perhaps as the pressure of completing work already underway made itself felt.

In 1937, after decades of building and buying enormous homes; purchasing vast amounts of art from Europe's castles and great houses, galleries here and abroad, estate sales and auctions; making movies; and expanding his journalistic empire, Hearst exhausted his personal fortune as well as his organization's finances.

Deaf to Ben Franklin's admonition, Hearst had been spending more than he had been making for years. On his collection alone it is estimated by some (probably inaccurately) that he spent about $50,000,000. On his New York City real estate alone another $50,000,000 was supposedly spent, which, at any other time, would have been viewed as a good investment, but in the depths of the

Depression, the mortgage payments on these properties were crushing. The love of his newspapers and the belief that he could magically resuscitate any failing newspaper had led him to hang on to papers that were losing millions annually.

When the records were put together and examined, they revealed that the financial anarchy loosed by Hearst had placed the organization into a staggering debt of $125,000,000. He had taken one of the most fecund financial empires and an enormous patrimony and had spent them both into chaos. A man of unquestioned brilliance and an unparalleled journalistic technician, he had breezily accumulated a personal debt larger than that of some nations at the time.

In June 1937, Hearst came to New York from San Simeon and did the hardest thing he ever had to do in his life. He surrendered personal financial control of the empire he had built to Clarence Shearn, counsel for the Chase National Bank, one of the 28 banks holding Hearst notes. He also took a cut in salary.

A committee of conservation was appointed from the organization's pool of executives, including W. R. Hearst, Jr., to attempt to save this dying corporate body by cutting away at those limbs and organs that were killing it. Hearst would have to give up as much as possible, give up the movies, give up the real estate, give up some of the newspapers, and, ultimately, give up two-thirds of his collection. All aspects of the man's empire that could not show a profit were to be sold in the desperate struggle to save something for the creditors, noteholders, and shareholders.

The great buyer, perhaps the greatest accumulator of them all, was now, in the midst of the Great Depression, forced to sell much that he had bought years before. The unseen, but coveted, contents of two Bronx warehouses, the motion picture studio, his beloved incunabula, radio stations, St. Donat's Castle, and square blocks of New York were all offered up in order to rescue the organization from impending bankruptcy. The committee was ruthless, doing what it had to do over a period of years. Selling the Clarendon, for instance, in the Depression was almost impossible; they let it go for a song. Better the staggering loss than the continuing mortgage payments.

A tremor went through the art world when rumors were heard that the Hearst vaults would be opened and their contents offered at auction. The contents were the motherlode of a collector's fantasy; works by Rembrandt and Hals, silver, the world's greatest private tapestry collection were to be auctioned, most at prices well below what Hearst had paid.

The unparalleled silver collection at St. Donat's was sold at Sotheby's in 1937 and at Christie's in London in 1938, and brought in one half of what Hearst had paid for it, which, considering it was 1938, was not really bad. Parke Bernet, which he had helped fatten, sold his collection of manuscripts, books, papers, and autographs. His collection of rooms, panelling, ceilings, windows, doors, and other bits and pieces that he had not used in his various constructions were sold off by Parish-Watson & Co. from a five-story building leased especially for the sale.

The battle for solvency went on from 1937 to 1942. In 1941, Armand Hammer arranged with Gimbel's department store in New York to use one of their floors for the sale of any part of the collection that could be sold on time, with terms. Over 100,000 square feet were crammed with objects for the curious to examine and the acquisitive to purchase. To Hearst, now 75 years old, it must have seemed that an evil spirit had taken up residence in the castle. He had been stripped of power and stripped of pride before all his gleeful critics.

The war that ended the Depression also ended the travails of the corporation. The thirst for news, full employment, and rising advertising and circulation saved the remainder of the Hearst publishing empire as well as that of the collection. The foreign entanglements of World War II, which Hearst had argued so vehemently against, ironically saved his fortune. It came at a time when the committee to conserve that fortune had its back against the wall. Selling art works in a country at war was not the way to get top dollar. However, the insatiable desire for news boosted circulation enormously, and the committee's efforts toward fiscal responsibility in all areas were starting to pay off. Hearst was in his eighties at the close of the war and, after all he had been through, the humiliation of having had to borrow money, the glare of publicity, and the grief of so much loss, he was still not through building. He resumed construction on the new wing of Casa Grande as soon as some money began to flow again.

Hearst and Marion Davies had spent some of the war years, 1942 through 1944, at his Northern California retreat, Wyntoon. They moved to the 67,000-acre estate from San Simeon to save money and to avoid the possibility of a coastal shelling by Japanese submarines. Where San Simeon was clear light and sparkle, Wyntoon, set in a deep forest wilderness, was a brooding "Bavarian village," consisting of three houses designed by Morgan, built to replace one large five-story house designed by Maybeck which had burned to the ground in 1929. Because they were a long way from Los Angeles and they were still short of money, Hearst was unable to populate the place with the retinue of show-business people that provided Marion with much of her diversion at the ranch. Marion was lonely, and Hearst was impatient to get back.

Sometime in the winter of 1944–45 they returned to San Simeon. It had been over eight years since Hearst had been able to indulge his construction mania. His sons, having achieved positions of power in the business and knowing the old man's ways, opposed further construction. Opposing further construction was one thing; denying it entirely to their father was another matter. They did, however, apply the brakes of fiscal reason and kept him from initiating another orgy of building. Left unfettered, he undoubtedly would have completed old plans, developed new ones, and spent himself into penury once more. Having no choice, they let him finish the interior of the new wing, which had been started in the 1920s and partly finished in the 1930s.

Construction did not fully start again until 1945. Morgan was 72 years old when she had her office resume work on the Enchanted Hill. She assigned the task to one of her assistants, Warren McClure. Her office prepared drawings and supervised work through 1946 and 1947, but age was finally starting to tell on her, and the job of finishing the wing fell to McClure. In 1948, Julia Morgan closed her office and retired from the practice of architecture.

At the start of the war, Casa Grande was complete; except for some changes in the furnishings, it was substantially as we see it today. The new wing's interior, however, was largely incomplete. As with everything else on the hill the wing had undergone a number of physical and design metamorphoses, as indicated by the existing drawings. McClure's task was to finish the second, third, and fourth floors; the ground floor, containing the Theater, was not touched. Those three upper floors had been left in various stages of completion. He did some alterations to the second floor, kept the plan of the third floor much as it was, and most radically altered the fourth floor, ripping out existing construction and rebuilding.

At either end of the wing on the fourth floor were bedrooms with uncompleted rooms between them. The bedrooms were connected by an exterior loggia which ran the length of the wing. Enclosing this loggia in 1947, McClure created one of the more curious rooms on the hill; it is a bathroom that is 6½ feet wide and 36 feet long. He shaped this space into a stunning example of the Art Deco style. In a curious way, it is one of the most original rooms in the complex. In fact, it is in the Main Building's bathrooms that the 20th century is allowed to exist unmolested by the collection and, as a result, many of them are first-rate examples of streamline design.

Warren McClure's work on the wing is an interesting and effective contrast to the early stylistic approach. Much simpler than the building's other parts, the wing evidences McClure's restrained attitude to interior design, which reflected a change of design attitude within the profession and possibly the fiscally restraining hand of Hearst's sons. This simplicity works to allow the very fine pieces in the wing to be seen to advantage and studied without distraction.

Opposite: The new wing takes on an exotic Moorish aspect in its top-floor rooms. Here, a Spanish ceiling of geometric design hovers over a bedroom alcove. A Kashan carpet hangs on the wall behind the Italian bed; on the floor is a coarser, yet equally decorative, Heriz carpet.

Left: Marble, late Art Deco plumbing and lighting fixtures, and extravagant use of space make this and other bathrooms in the new wing the most interesting of any on the estate.

Below: White walls, red tile floors, Spanish ceilings, and carved doors are characteristic of the new wing. A 17th-century Peruvian armorial tapestry, a Chinese vase lamp from the Marion Davies collection, and an unusual Portuguese table in English taste are among the decorative objects in the second-floor main sitting room.

Flat and unelaborated plastered white walls display the exceptional antiques in a much more familiar (to us) and contemporary manner. The rooms certainly look more like galleries than the rest of the house, having about them a cleaner, less intensely personal look and feel.

Although it is said that Hearst planned to move into the wing, it was never occupied, and perhaps this explains the sense of abandonment and of expectation it gives. The rooms have never been charged by Hearst's electricity or that of the people with whom he surrounded himself.

Watching the work begin again on the new wing could only have put Hearst in mind of the days of earlier work. In his middle age, he had been filled with prodigious vigor, ready always for a public scrap, a new venture, and actively designing his environment. As a man who always looked ahead, it could not have but saddened him somewhat to look back. The old friends and adversaries were no longer alive: Arthur Brisbane, Will Rogers, Al Smith, Joseph Pulitzer, Flo Ziegfeld, and Orrin Peck. Julia Morgan was still alive but no longer on the hill working excitedly with him. The two of them were unable to continue what they had begun together. Living a long time, he had the advantage of seeing and making a lot of life; the disadvantage was that he outlived most of that life.

Morgan, now retired, began to indulge her love of travel. While visiting abroad, she would make notes and sketches which she would add to her correspondence with Hearst. It must have served to nourish these remarkable elderly friends to continue to work, however haltingly, on a project they both knew they would never see completed and to correspond about ideas, foreign places, and architecture.

Hearst was begrudgingly allowed by his sons to continue his mania at a deliberately slow pace. That pace probably did not bother him too much since he never would have allowed himself to finish the project anyhow. Morgan knew this as well and had come to terms with it years before. He never did allow her to put a permanent roof on any part of Casa Grande precisely because of the finality that act would have represented.

Sometime in mid-1947 his heart, which doctors had been cautioning him about for years, suffered from a severe fibrillation. His physicians cautioned him once more: to stay on the hill in his condition, away from adequate medical facilities, would be tempting death. He and his companion Marion Davies reluctantly decided to move to Los Angeles. They moved into a house in Beverly Hills after making the painful final trip down the road from La Cuesta Encantada. Hearst was not just leaving his home; he was, in a way, leaving his life. Although he was to live four more years, a part of him surely died when he realized he would never see his Enchanted Hill again.

SAN SIMEON:
THE COLLECTION

 VISITORS TO SAN SIMEON, confronted by what remains of Hearst's awesome compulsion to collect, might infer that they are in the presence of some wholly unique and extraordinary personal statement. To a degree that inference would be correct; it would also be mistaken to the same degree. The compulsion to collect art was shared by many other late 19th- and early 20th-century capitalists. Art, it was romantically thought at the time, was the other side of the mirror of their daily world. Where those capitalists fought and grappled in the financial gutter, artists soared among clouds of virtue; where they plundered the resources of the earth for profit, art was pure of motive. Many collected because they held the peculiarly American notion that art, while delightful and engaging, was morally good, a tonic for the soul.

There is a degree of exploitation involved in setting the price of any commodity, but the price of a piece of art, alone among all goods, is solely and innately an index of want. The only measurable quality of art that bears any relationship to an economic system based on supply and demand is its rarity.

The wealthy families of the 19th and 20th centuries had two things in common: the general means by which they accumulated their money and how they spent it—they almost all supported the art market. The bulk of items for sale, mainly from Europe and the Far East, were usually put together by the auction houses as well as

Opposite: At intervals along the Esplanade are groupings of statuary, columns, and, in four instances, ancient Roman sarcophagi of which this 3rd-century example, the "Apollo and the Muses" sarcophagus, is the finest. Its condition is remarkable considering the intricacy of the carving and high relief of the figures and details on the front panel.

galleries whose agents, touring Europe and dealing through local contacts, would acquire an entire room, tapestries, silver, furniture, sculpture, books, paintings, screens, or whatever in different places, and when lucky, the entire contents of a home. These items were paid for by advances (sometimes as high as $500,000) given to the agent by the auction house or private dealer.

These art objects flowed in a ceaseless stream from Europe through the auction houses of New York and into the homes of the wealthy across the country. Unfortunately, the constant demand for such a volume of goods spawned an antiques industry in Europe that increasingly flooded the market with fakes. Many of these fakes, plus works of art with false attributions, found their way into many American collections, including Hearst's.

For years it has been fashionable to describe the process that brought so much of Europe's art to this country as a form of looting, or cultural plundering. In a way it was, but, in fairness, it must be said that the process was, at the same time, an act of wholesale preservation.

These antiques and art objects were not always sold out of economic necessity; they were also sold out of ignorance and, more often, indifference. It is not that the sellers did not know that the work had value so much as it seems they ceased caring about it— there was so much of it around, who could care for it all?

Most of these hidden collections were properly attributed, catalogued, restored, studied and seen only after they had been sold to English and American dealers. The dealers who bought the work and restored it for future sale preserved vast amounts of work that otherwise would no doubt have been further decimated by neglect and, in too many instances, lost forever.

Auction houses and galleries also recycled works from American collections that were sold as part of estate settlements. One such sale was the auction of the Yerkes collection in 1910. Charles Tyson Yerkes was one of the quintessential 19th-century capitalists who romped through life with a gift for making large amounts of money, often through thievery (he served a sentence after a conviction for stock manipulation), and a talent for spending it as well. He built and furnished four magnificent homes—one for each of the women he lived with—and he bought art. He spent incredible amounts on both good and inferior pieces, and it must be said in his favor that his taste improved with age while that of many of his contempories did not.

In April 1910, when part of his collection went under the auctioneer's hammer, it promised to be one of the largest and richest auctions ever held. Yerkes had owned what was at the time the finest collection of 16th- and 17th-century Oriental rugs in the world. He had work by Hals, Rembrandt, Turner, Corot, Van Dyck, and Raphael.

*Detail of the "Apollo and the Muses"
sarcophagus showing three of the Muses.*

Among the items in the auction catalogue that were sold to Hearst
was item no. 255, Antique Greek Marble Sarcophagus, which is
actually Roman, dating from between 230 and 240 A.D. Now opposite House B on the Esplanade at San Simeon, it is one of the most
notable and impressive pieces in the collection. The carved figures
represent Apollo and Minerva in the center of the front panel with
the Muses to each side. Apollo is identified by the tripod altar next to
him around which a snake is wrapped. The figures are carved in high
relief and are somewhat static in composition. The eyes, hair, and
corners of the mouths are deeply drilled to accentuate the carving, a
typical Roman technique, but done especially well here.

The long, beautifully proportioned sarcophagus was not used to
hold the dead in a mummified state. The body was placed within it
with quicklime to hasten decomposition, prevent putrefaction, and
stop disease. In a monograph written for The Metropolitan Museum
of Art, which owns a similar piece, Anna McCann wrote, "Perhaps
the sarcophagus was originally intended for a poet or dramatist who
chose this lively theme in which to clothe his own eschatological
hopes."[22]

The sarcophagus first turns up in documentation ascribing its ownership to Don Maffeo, Prince of Colonna of Sciarra, Italy. It was one of the many items which, in 1811, he divided between his son and his cousin. From 1811 on, there is no record until it is mentioned in the 1910 Yerkes auction catalogue. The sarcophagus surfaces again in Hearst's records where it is noted that it was shipped from the Clarendon apartment to San Simeon in 1921. The correspondence among the papers of Julia Morgan at The California Polytechnic State University, San Luis Obispo, records that Hearst bought it in the 1910 sale.

Tracing the provenance of a work of art and authenticating its passage is a serious undertaking. Like a voyage of exploration, it is an endeavor in which much geography is charted and studied while large areas of terra incognita remain on the map. The work of tracing the provenance of all of the pieces on the hill was begun by Taylor Coffman in 1972. It is work of persistence, detection, patience, scholarship, and luck. The "Apollo and the Muses" sarcophagus is a good example of this process.

Julia Morgan's office was responsible for cataloguing the part of Hearst's collection that was in California, so that she would know what was available for use on the hill. According to the taped recollections of two of Morgan's employees, they worked in the warehouses at the Pleasanton Hacienda and the village of San Simeon supervising the uncrating of objects: "We would set them up and then I would stand with a yardstick alongside to give it scale and Sam Crow would take a picture. Then we would give it a number and I would write a brief description of it. These were eventually all enlarged and made into albums, and there were shelves of these photographs. When Mr. Hearst would write and say, I want a Florentine mantel in Cottage C in Room B and four yards of tiles, then we would look it up in the books and find something that would fit."[23] In fact, the descriptions of the objects were copied from sales catalogues and dealers' invoices. Morgan's employees did not have the necessary knowledge of art to catalogue them on their own.

Hearst did not have to be personally present at an auction to bid. The major houses in New York—Anderson Galleries, The American Art Association Galleries, and later Parke Bernet—printed elaborate catalogues with photographs and detailed descriptions of the objects of a particular sale. These catalogues, some of them distinguished works of scholarship, were then sent to Hearst and others whom the auction house knew to be avid collectors. Hearst, after studying the contents, would then either attend the auction or assign an agent to act for him on those preselected items, stipulating a ceiling price only.

Because of the volume of his purchases, Hearst became a favorite

Above: A 1920s Art Deco silver night lamp from Tiffany & Co. Below: Lovebirds decorate an Art Deco glass lamp by an unknown designer and manufacturer.

of European and American art dealers. He was an eager participant in the market and would naturally become disappointed and sometimes angry if a particular item eluded him at an auction after the bidding had gone beyond the top price he had been willing to pay. The setting of a ceiling price was a specific instruction relative to an item; occasionally his instructions to his agents were less defined though certainly more humorous, as on the occasion when he went after some silverware and told his agent to "pay anything reasonably extortionate."[24]

Hearst, as other collectors, often came up against the problem of the auctioneers and dealers attempting to run the price of an object up in bidding by having house shills bid against them. No doubt this practice as well as his desire did cause him occasionally to pay extravagantly for a particular item, but there is no evidence to support the popularly held myth that because of his greed he paid, in his lifetime, upwards of twice the value of his holdings. In fact, a much closer scrutiny of the records of purchases reveals the opposite: the greater part of the pieces in his collection were acquired for upper three- and lower four-figure dollar amounts. The single most expensive piece on the hill is a millefleur tapestry for which Hearst paid $100,000.

Hearst did not buy in ignorance. He was well grounded in the arts and continually studied them. He was knowledgeable about armor, at one time having the finest collection in the world, and was possessed of excellent taste and judgment about tapestries, rugs, architecture, silver, and antiques in general. But his rash and oceanic urges led him to buy voluminously. Mitchell Samuels, of French and Company, tried time and again to curb those urges, to caution Hearst, and yet, according to Samuels, he supposedly bought over $8,000,000 worth of furniture, tapestries, and miscellaneous objects from him alone. He was an inexorable buyer; the sheer number of his purchases helped to warp the economics of the art world of two continents.

His apartment at the Clarendon groaned with art works. He had warehouses at San Simeon and stored art at the Pleasanton ranch as well until he sold the Hacienda in the mid-1920s. At Southern Boulevard and 143rd Street in the Bronx, he owned two five-story warehouses that covered the entire block and were filled with his purchases. Here were stored the silly, the curious, the sublime works he had purchased for millions of dollars: scores of statues, thousands of rare books, entire English rooms and halls, a legion of suits of armor, furniture, wellheads, doorways, window frames, and of course, the ultimate folly of his Spanish purchases, an entire 12th-century Cistercian monastery from the remote village of Sacramenia, Spain, bought in the 1920s.

Overleaf: In the Billiard Room is a mille-fleur tapestry of uncommonly provincial design—an ideal choice of naive, lightly romantic subject matter appropriate to San Simeon. It is undetermined whether the tapestry is an original Gothic piece or a later interpretation of such work.

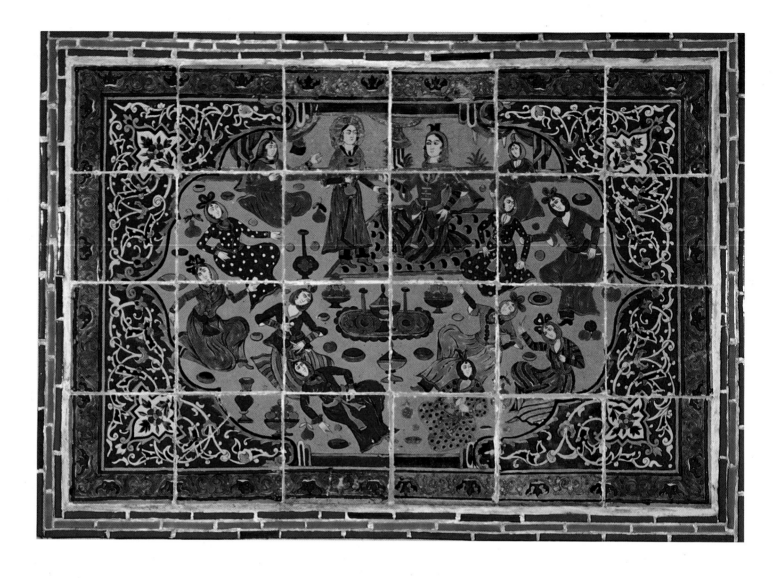

Above: The Billiard Room is the setting for an extensive display of Persian tile pictures. The five tile fields in the room are from the Safavid period and originally decorated palaces in Ispahan.

Left: An antique stone lintel and contemporary doors are combined to form a Gothic-style doorway that leads from the Billiard Room to the North Duplex suites. A pair of 14th-century lions guard the passageway.

One of the collection's most painstakingly decorated objects is the Billiard Room's French Renaissance jewel cabinet, made in 1562 of ebony, with Limoges enamel plaques distributed on its architectural façade.

Two of five Hearst-era warehouses in San Simeon village. The wood structure, built in 1878 by George Hearst, was used through the 1940s as the "freight shed" for art objects, furniture, and building materials. The white-stuccoed concrete building, frequently mistaken for a mission, was the last of the warehouses to be built, c. 1930.

The workmen who had to dismantle the 250 tons of stone that comprised the 700-year-old cloister were attacked a number of times by the furious villagers who naturally objected to what they viewed as an incredible act of piracy. Each stone had to be separately dismantled, numbered, and recorded for reassembling. Ten thousand five hundred individual crates were needed to pack the whole thing. Forty miles of road were built at Hearst's expense to get them to the nearest railroad, and a fleet of freighters was hired to transport them to New York, where they lay in a bleak warehouse, a gigantic, three-dimensional jigsaw puzzle never to be assembled. And he did not do it once; in 1931, he did it again at the urging of one of his favorite sources, the Bynes.

Arthur Byne and his wife, Mildred Stapley Byne, were a husband-and-wife team of impressive scholastic and persuasive abilities, able to convince collectors to buy all sorts of curious items. Authorities on the subject of Spanish antiquities, they functioned as free agents buying for Hearst, other collectors, and galleries. They were also brilliant at negotiating enormous pieces of the Spanish patrimony around customs officials and out of the country. It was the Bynes who had gotten Hearst many of his more important, larger Spanish pieces.

Julia Morgan had long held that there should be museums of architecture as well as museums of art. Her thought was to reconstruct a whole building of significant styles and have the building itself be the museum. Obviously Hearst agreed with her and, with the Bynes' connivance, bought the Spanish monastery, Santa Maria de Ovila, near the town of Siguenza. It, too, was carefully dismantled, stone by stone, each stone numbered, marked, and then taken by mule, oxcart, and railway to Madrid and diligently packed in numbered wooden crates. The thousands of crates were moved again to 12 chartered freighters that took them to San Francisco.

Hearst gave the monastery to the M. H. de Young Memorial Museum but did not provide funds to erect the building. Some years later, a fire destroyed many of the crates and their markings, reducing the neat stack of stones to a heap of rubble. Time, weather, neglect, and vandalism have rendered the stones useless, and today they lie in Golden Gate Park in San Francisco.

Curiously, by the mid-1930s, Hearst had developed a notion that was certainly contradictory to his actions. From Spain, in 1934, Hearst wrote: "A good part of Spain is being transferred to America. We get some of it. More goes to the museums, and much into private hands. In the picture books of Ronda there is a beautiful hall with a glorious ceiling. We wanted to see it. Alas, the ceiling had been taken down, the hall demolished. What happened to it? Oh, it went to America, etcetera. I know I get some of the things, but Spain ought to be like Italy and keep their important things in important places, because that is what brings the tourists, and the tourists are about all that is profitable in Spain."[25] The sentiment, while reasonable, did not, however, affect his purchasing.

Hearst's predominantly Spanish and Italian collection at San Simeon is visually impressive, and more importantly, thematically and stylistically unified. It offers us a clear indication that while Hearst was not a religious man, he certainly must have found some deep consonance with the essential message of what were, for the most part, products of a Catholic disposition. Most art prior to the 18th century was commissioned either by the church itself or by individuals who shared, along with the artists and society at large, the dominant themes of the time in Italy and Spain—mainly religious—which were expressed in a historical or mythological manner. Although this indicates what was available, it does not completely explain that part of his collection he chose to live with.

The collection in its entirety is impressive for its size certainly, for the quality of many of the pieces, and the number of categories in which Hearst collected; but most of all it stands out for the manner in which the collection and the architecture were fused. Although much of the collection was sold during, as well as after, his lifetime, the character of the collection can still be seen in what remains, especially where Hearst's selectivity is mirrored by Julia Morgan's in the manner in which she combined objects at La Cuesta Encantada.

Consideration of the architecture at San Simeon can only be marginally separated from consideration of much of the collection. The architecture was influenced to a lesser degree than is believed by what was available of the very best in the collection. The sizes of the tapestries, choir stalls, ceilings, mantels, and other objects in relation to one another did cause the larger rooms and bedroom suites to be viewed as armatures for the hanging and application of decoration and certain specific pieces. But this is not to lessen Julia Morgan's efforts. In all instances when combining pieces from the collection with each other or with new work that had to be fabricated she demonstrated her own excellent taste. Most of the ceilings and many of the built-in objects from the collection—panelling or choir stalls—had to undergo some alteration. The Assembly Room, for example, large enough to contain tapestries, would have to have had the ceiling chosen for it, cut to fit if too large, or enlarged if too small. Any of that work was done on the site by the resident craftsmen or in studios in the Bay Area. The rooms on the hill were infrequently designed and built to fit the dimensions of specific preselected objects.

The removal of works of decorative art such as ceilings, doors, or even statuary from their original locations and modifying them for use as decor has been questioned by some. As an acceptable and widespread practice, it dates from the latter half of the 16th century in Italy where there existed an intense interest in collecting archeological pieces and combining them in new work. This produced a decorative style which transformed the façades and interiors of buildings into showcases of contrasts of style, scale, and content. The Villa Medici in Rome is a fine example of that practice.

The practice almost certainly changes the contextual integrity of the piece but that need not mean that it is entirely violated. Certainly no more so than a contemporary example: the façade of the old United States Branch Bank in the Garden Court of the American Wing of The Metropolitan Museum of Art in New York. The façade cannot be viewed as architecture any longer since it is essentially two-dimensional and is totally lacking context. At best, it is viewed as what it is, a large archeological fragment and, at worst, a decorative abstraction. However, it is on display; would it be better not seen at all for reasons of aesthetic purity?

Much more of the architectural decoration was produced on the site than is commonly understood. The craftsmen worked mainly from the drawings of Thaddeus Joy, one of Julia Morgan's associates. These full-size drawings derived their inspiration, or were copied, from many of the design source books in Morgan's library on Spanish-Moorish, Italian Renaissance, or Spanish colonial architecture that were so popular nationally. Most of the designs for the

Detail of one of several bays from an Andalusian convent ceiling installed in the new wing. The individual rectangular panels are decorated in Gothic lettering with the initials of Christ on alternating grounds of pale green and orange.

ceilings in the smaller houses, for example, were the work of Joy, executed in cast plaster by Theodore Van de Loo and his son, John, who worked on the hill for 23 years. The craftsmen who worked on the site were so skilled that the work they did went unrecognized for years; much of it was thought, instead, to be antiques from the collection.

The most pointed example of this is the teak gable that stretches across the front of Casa Grande between the two towers. For years it had been claimed by the tour guides that the gable came from a palace in Peru. Examination reveals no substantial evidence to justify that claim. Teak grows in abundance in the East Indies and in Southeast Asia but not in South America. It would appear improbable that the original colonial carvers would have used a foreign wood for a work of such large dimensions rather than mahogany or any other suitable native wood that they used everywhere else.

Every major gallery and collector was importing and collecting work from the Old World, from the Orient to a lesser degree, and relatively little from South America. If the story were true, it would be one of the very few existing pieces from South America visible in the entire Hearst collection and, as such, just seems too unlikely.

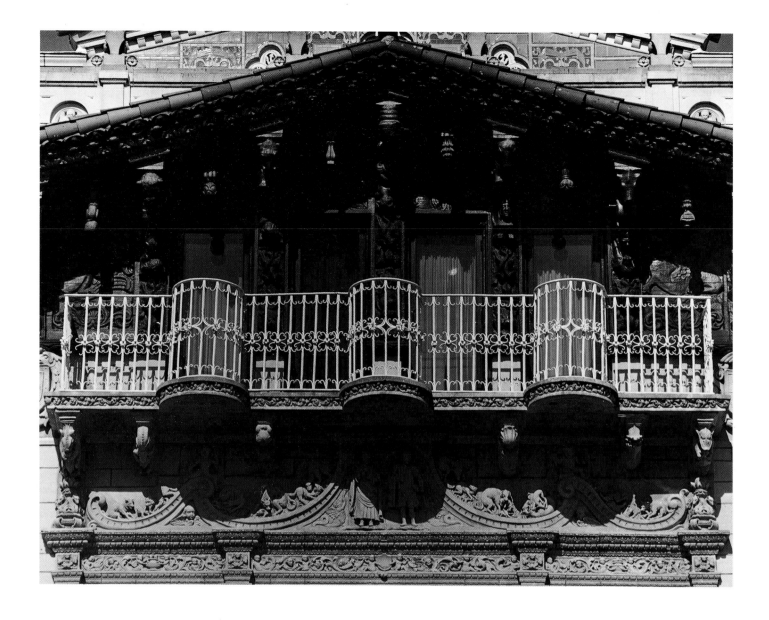

Jules Suppo's teak gable on the third level of Casa Grande's main façade.

One possibility for which there is some evidence is that Jules Suppo of San Francisco—the principal wood carver—based the design on three original panels (very likely from Spain) depicting bears and rosettes, and carved the rest of the gable to match. The evidence—a photo of Suppo alongside three old-looking sections—is, however, slight. The photo may have been taken after he had already carved those sections—in fact, carved the entire gable himself—using as his motif the California bear, a bit of whimsy Hearst certainly would have appreciated.

The whole Peruvian myth, on the other hand, may have been started by Hearst himself in one of his mirthful moods, casually telling someone in jest an improbable story (which he enjoyed doing) of how he acquired it from Peru. The point here is that the craftsmen did incredible work, creating wholly new pieces as well as matching old work. Nowhere did they do it better than in the bedroom suites of Casa Grande and its four major rooms: the Assembly Room, the Refectory, the Library, and Hearst's Gothic Suite.

Stretching the entire length of the front of the Main Building, the Assembly Room, 83 feet long, 31 feet wide, and 22 feet high, is the largest room in the house. Here, in this generously proportioned space, the guests would gather and enjoy cocktails while waiting for an hour or two till their host joined them, before taking dinner in the Refectory, usually at 9:00 P.M.

Above them, as they sat and chatted on overstuffed chairs or perhaps played with jigsaw puzzles, or had a social game of cards at a 16th-century walnut Italian table, hung fine examples of the European weaving arts—two sets of "Scipio Africanus" tapestries and the "Triumph of Religion" tapestry. The set of four large "Scipio Africanus" tapestries, hung on the two long walls of the room, were designed by Giulio Romano, an Italian artist and architect of the 16th century given to a violent and ironic stylistic manner, and woven by Flemish craftsmen around 1550. The tapestries depict key events from the Second Punic Wars between Rome and Carthage. Scipio, the general who led the Roman armies to victory, is recognizable in each panel; he is depicted draped in a blue robe with white stars. Hearst acquired these four tapestries from French and Company, in 1921, for $65,000, not an excessive amount to pay for works of such quality. A year earlier, however, at The American Art Association Galleries, he successfully bid only $6,000 for another of his finer pieces, the "Triumph of Religion." Hung on the north wall of the room, the tapestry was designed by the 17th-century Flemish painter, Peter Paul Rubens. It is a volcanic representation of Roman Catholic dogma and a profound witness of faith. Typically Rubensesque, its sheer size, its pictorial conception which treats the figures not as surface pattern but as solid masses existing in space, and the sure handling of complex and dynamic spatial movements make it one of the most impressive items in an already impressive room. The second set of five smaller "Scipio Africanus" tapestries, also by Giulio Romano, is represented on the south wall of the room by "The Burning of the Numidian Camp."

Just below the tapestries on the long east wall, flanking both sides of the fireplace, there are two sets of Italian carved walnut choir stalls. To the right of the fireplace, hardly distinguishable from the stalls, is the door through which Hearst would lead his guests to dinner. The Assembly Room, more than any of the others, best represents the essential characteristics of Hearst's collection because of its scale and the quality and juxtaposition of the furnishings. It is not, as are other major rooms or suites, thematic; that is, it does not seek to echo a particular style; but rather, it is a dignified room, vaguely Renaissance, furnished with some of the best pieces in the collection and a miscellaneous group of silver candlesticks, statuary, odd columns, Oriental rugs, cases, an electric player piano, and an

outrageously excessive 19th-century silver oil lamp, possibly from the collection of Phoebe Hearst.[26] On the 16th-century Italian table in the center of the room sits one of the more exquisite art objects in the collection. It is a presentation case or perhaps a reliquary. Made of ebony, gilt bronze, cut-and-polished rock crystal, and semiprecious stones, it was given to Hearst by Mitchell Samuels of French and Company in 1927. There is a strong possibility that it dates from the late 16th or early 17th century and is from France.

Under the extensively restored carved wood 16th-century ceiling from the Palazzo Martinengo in Brescia, Italy, the Assembly Room's grouping of disparate elements and styles achieves a kind of curious harmony because of the respectful consideration Hearst gave to the architecture in relation to the most casual items; items, one would think, a client would not bother to involve the architect with. In a message to Julia Morgan, Hearst wrote: "I think we should have in

"The Burning of the Numidian Camp" is one of a set of five smaller Brussels tapestries at San Simeon, woven in the 16th century from designs by Giulio Romano. The subject is the epic battles and confrontations of Scipio Africanus, the Roman General, and Hannibal, the Carthaginian, during the Second Punic War. In this panel, the Romans are shown in an early morning attack on the enemy's camp. Flanking the tapestry are two of Albert Bertel Thorvaldsen's four medallions.

the assembly room, two enormous divans the full width of the window, very deep and low, but with short backs so the window will not be encroached upon."[27]

The room also contains the work of two neoclassical sculptors: Albert Bertel Thorvaldsen (1770–1844), a Dane who studied in Rome, and Antonio Canova (1757–1822). Canova was a sculptor who worked in Rome and had an enormous influence on the artists of his day. His "Venus" at the north end of the room is typically neoclassical. While painterly in conception, its sculptural mass creates an illusion whereby the very substance of the white marble takes on an air of deliquescent coolness. William Permain, Hearst's agent in England, bought the statue at the auction of the Landsdowne Marbles held at Christie's in London in 1930.

From the Assembly Room, Hearst and his guests would walk to the adjacent Refectory for dinner. The Refectory was the only dining room on the hill and dinner the only meal Hearst insisted be taken communally. Breakfast was available there from 9:00 A.M. to noon, and a buffet lunch was also served in the Refectory from 2:00 to 4:00 P.M., accommodating the casual recreational schedules each guest chose to keep. Dinner, however, was somewhat formal and sometimes the one time during the day Hearst saw his guests.

Seating at the four separate Italian refectory tables was by place card; the luckier of the guests were seated around Hearst and Marion

The French Renaissance rock crystal cabinet of the 16th century, variously identified as a reliquary, jewel casket, and presentation case, which sits on a table in the Assembly Room. Photograph Robert A. Hanks; courtesy Hearst San Simeon State Historical Monument.

Davies in the center of the 67-foot-long room. A section of the room is almost square (28 feet wide by 27 feet high), and, like the Assembly Room, it is hung with tapestries and lined with choir stalls. The stalls are from the Cathedral of Urgel in Spain and date from the 15th century. The ceiling is probably Italian from the 16th century. Here, under the light of electric chandeliers that sparkled and reflected off the stunning collection of Mexican and Flemish candlesticks, Irish and English silver dishes and warming plates, the guests would read the evening's dinner selection and the title of the evening movie from a menu printed daily. Along the north wall, on the table under the 16th-century Flemish tapestry illustrating events from the life of Daniel, is an exceptional group of silver objects. There are four elaborate Flemish neoclassical (1770s) candlesticks, an oval English wine cistern, and perhaps the finest silver piece on the hill, a beautifully chased and intricately worked parliamentary mace made in Dublin in 1867. Hearst purchased it at a Parke Bernet auction in September 1946.

The room, a favorite of Hearst's and one of the most evocatively theatrical in the house, was to have had stained glass in the upper windows of both side walls. Hearst changed his mind, realizing that at night the stained glass would be visually mute. Instead, he introduced the flags of the districts of Siena whose brilliant colors and bold designs would sparkle both during the day and in artificial illumination.

Seated in 22 chairs that are in most cases reproductions of a 16th-century Italian "Dante" chair, the guests could enjoy not only the exquisitely furnished and proportioned room, reverberant with echoes of medieval nobility, but the superb food, the finest champagne, attentive service, scintillating company, and the curiosity that among the fine china and silver on the antique table were also paper napkins and ketchup, mustard, and other condiments in their original bottles—sentimental reminders of those early camping trips Hearst took with his father, and later with his wife and sons, to this spot when it was nothing but rock, sky, oak trees, and sea.

Perhaps the most comfortably elegant room in Casa Grande is the subdued and beautifully proportioned Library above the Assembly

The finest neoclassical sculpture at San Simeon is the Assembly Room's "Venus" by the Venetian sculptor Antonio Canova. The sculpture was formerly in the Lansdowne collection into which it passed from Lucien Bonaparte, the original owner. Opposite: Flamboyant Gothic tracery decorates the shallow canopy sections of the Refectory's set of 15th-century choir stalls from the Cathedral of Urgel in Spain.

Overleaf
Left: Two of the finest categories in the Hearst collection—silver and tapestry—are well represented in the Refectory. On the north wall is an early 16th-century Flemish tapestry showing the prophet Daniel in the court of Nebuchadnezzar. Flemish, English, and Irish silver objects occupy the side table. Two 18th-century Mexican silver candlesticks are displayed on the dining tables along with four place settings of English china and even ketchup and mustard to give an idea of how life once was at the "ranch." Right above: A Queen Anne wine cistern of 1710, made by the Huguenot silversmith, David Willaume, is part of the silver display in the Refectory. Courtesy Hearst San Simeon State Historical Monument. Right center: Late 19th-century mace from Dublin, Ireland, in the Refectory. Courtesy Hearst San Simeon State Historical Monument. Right below: One of the Refectory's eight silver candlesticks by the Antwerp silversmith, Michel Verbiest, dated 1774–75. Photograph Dean Hurd, Impact Pictures.

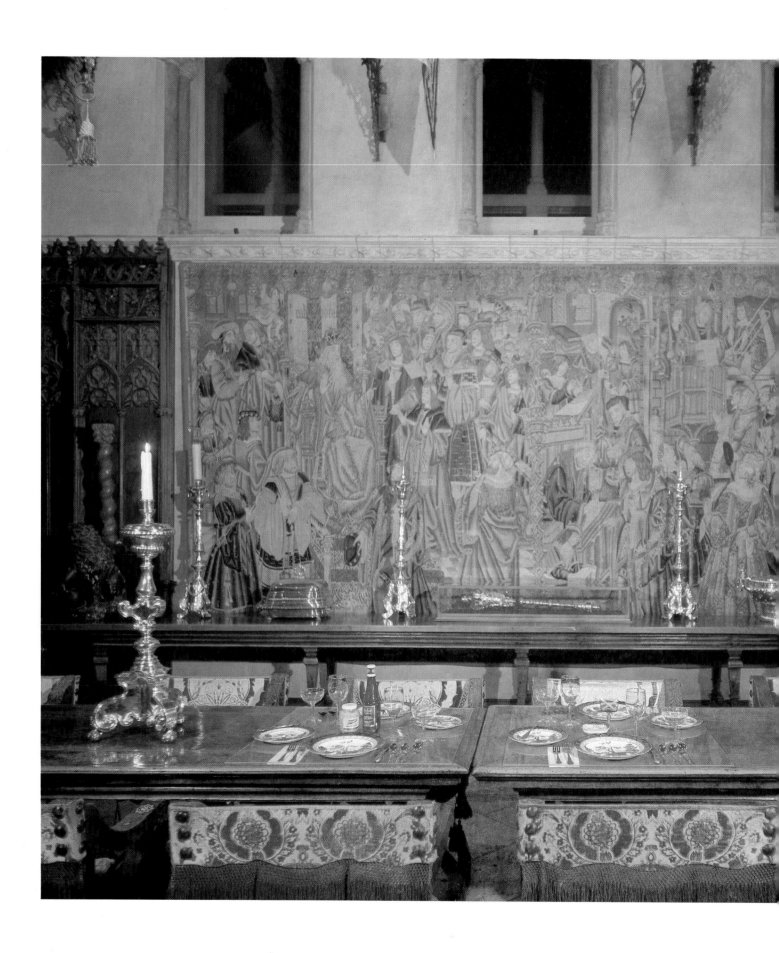

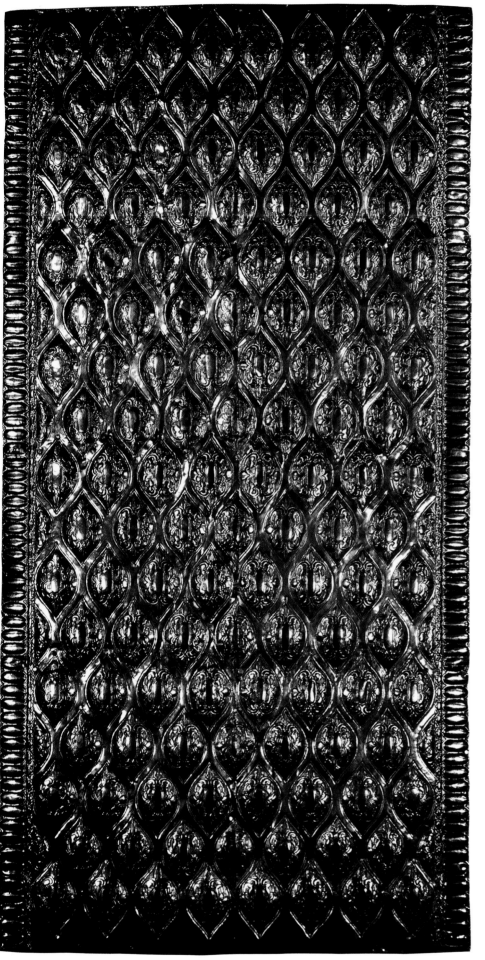

The left-hand leaf of a two-part door now serves as a wall decoration in the new wing. The paper-thin silver repoussé is typical 17th-century Spanish work.

Room, which guests were free to use. It was in this room that Hearst kept many favorites from his book collection. The room is lined with beautifully made wood cabinets containing approximately 4,500 volumes ranging in subject matter from popular novels of the time to works on philosophy, religion, history, science, biography, art, general reference books, and 17th-century rare books. It must have been a popular room for those disposed to serenity. The sun streaming in the west windows and reflected off the wood surfaces suffuses the room with a soft, gold-brown light that complements the room's contents. The deeply coffered Spanish ceiling is from the 16th century and comes from the state apartments in the Castle Benies, province of Aragon. It is the major unifying element in a room whose furnishings are intimate in size and scale, disparate in style, and encouraging of close scrutiny. Displayed are such pieces as 16th- and 17th-century Italian and Spanish tables, small bronzes and busts, among which is a 2nd-century-B.C. Greco-Roman two-headed marble bust which was used as the model for the lamp standards around the Neptune Pool.

The Library also contains the remainder of Hearst's superb collection of Greek vases. It was one of the most extensive and prized private collections in the world when it was intact. Though significantly reduced in number, it still remains one of the most important collections of its kind, and certainly ranks among the best private collections in the country. Between 1956 and 1963, 245 vases left the collection. In 1956, 66 were given to The Metropolitan Museum of Art in New York. The largest number of vases that left San Simeon at one time was 133, shipped east by the corporation to be included in the next-to-last Hearst-collection auction held at Parke Bernet on April 5–6, 1963. Randolph Hearst bought 28 vases from the San Simeon warehouses on January 22, 1962. The Walters Art Gallery in Baltimore was given four vases in 1958, and 14 vases were sold from the warehouses at various times to individuals and art dealers. The collection presently contains 156 vases. Almost every type, shape, and style of Greek vase is represented.

Hearst's private suite of rooms on the third floor was accessible by invitation only. On that floor is the Gothic Suite (bedrooms and sitting room) and the Gothic Study, his command post when in residence. The study is actually two rooms: an enormous library framed by pointed arches and lined with book shelves and cabinets and another smaller, more private room behind a fireplace. The end of the room is all glass, providing an incredible view beyond the courtyard of the Santa Lucia mountains and the rising sun. This enormous study was added after Hearst's bedrooms had been completed and a roof put over four bedrooms on the second floor.

The dominant design element is the series of pointed arches along

The north end of the second-floor Library with its decorative presentation of the Greek vase collection.

Right: Etruscan bronze cista (jewel or toiletries box), 3rd century B.C., in the Library. Courtesy Hearst San Simeon State Historical Monument. Below: Detail of a gilt and polychromed soffit in the Gothic Study's 15th-century ceiling from Campos, Spain.

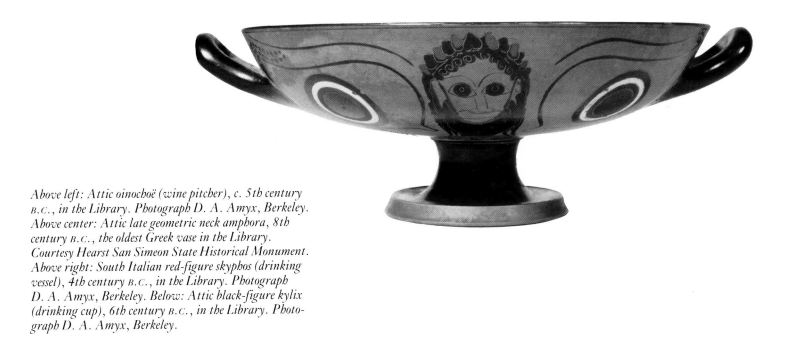

*Above left: Attic oinochoë (wine pitcher), c. 5th century
B.C., in the Library. Photograph D. A. Amyx, Berkeley.
Above center: Attic late geometric neck amphora, 8th
century B.C., the oldest Greek vase in the Library.
Courtesy Hearst San Simeon State Historical Monument.
Above right: South Italian red-figure skyphos (drinking
vessel), 4th century B.C., in the Library. Photograph
D. A. Amyx, Berkeley. Below: Attic black-figure kylix
(drinking cup), 6th century B.C., in the Library. Photo-
graph D. A. Amyx, Berkeley.*

the length of the room. The arches are painted in geometric patterns and mythological and biblical scenes. The decoration of the arches was done by Camille Solon, a decorator in Morgan's employ who worked at San Simeon off and on for some 15 years. It was from this room that Hearst, with his secretary Willicombe at his side, managed his enterprises, reviewing all of his newspapers till very early in the morning before retiring to his bedroom. This library contains some 7,500 volumes in categories that describe Hearst's major intellectual interests, the fine arts, biography, history, and philosophy. The library also contains most of the limited editions he purchased at important book sales in New York.

The bookcases that line the walls were built specifically for the room and contain not only books but many fine examples of smaller objets d'art, the finest of which is a 17th-century carved ivory German goblet, a well-proportioned piece covered with delightful carved allegorical figures. Over the fireplace that divides the study in two is a portrait of Hearst in his early thirties, painted in 1894 by his friend Orrin Peck. The portrait is riveting: young Hearst was an extremely handsome man who wore pale mustaches beneath a severe, straight bridge of a nose. Pale, icy blue eyes stare out, engaging and vaguely disturbing the viewer with their ferocious, penetrating intensity. The prominence given to the portrait is probably not so much the result of vanity on Hearst's part as a gesture of remembrance for his beloved friend.

Hearst's bedroom, the South Gothic Bedroom, is especially interesting because of the number of personal things that are displayed. The walls are hung with photographs of his parents and other personal memorabilia, as well as an excerpted poem that Hearst had specially printed. Adding the title "La Cuesta Encantada" to the lines of "The Lady from Lyons," by Sir Edward Bulwer Lytton, the poem is an apt evocation of the essence of the hill.

If thou wouldst have me paint
The home to which, could love fulfill its prayers
This hand would lead thee, listen . . . .

Hearst's South Gothic Bedroom is comparatively small and exceedingly monastic in tone. San Simeon's rarest and most unusual ceiling is installed here, a 14th-century example from Teruel, Spain, replete with Gothic iconography in the painted figures. Hanging from it is a 17th-century Italian silvered bronze lamp. Beneath the French Gothic bed is an Ispahan Meshed carpet; on the walls are pictures of George and Phoebe Hearst.

A palace lifting to eternal summer
Its marble walls, from out a gloss bower
Of coolest foliage musical with birds....

And when night came... the perfumed light
Stole through the mists of alabaster lamps,
And every air was heavy with the sighs
Of orange-groves and music from sweet lutes,
And murmurs of low fountains that gush forth
In the midst of roses!—Dost thou like the picture?

In the room is the most prized painting on the hill as well as the oldest. It is a Madonna and Child given to Hearst in 1932 by "Cissy" Patterson, publisher of the *Washington Times-Herald*. It had been believed to be the work of Segna di Bonaventura, a 14th-century Sienese painter who was a follower of Duccio di Buoninsegna (1278–c.1319), founder of the Sienese school, but Burton B. Fredericksen of the J. Paul Getty Museum, in his *Handbook of the Paintings in the Hearst San Simeon State Historical Monument*, wrote, "the quality is exceptionally high and close to the master himself...." It is a Sienese masterwork with a characteristically generous use of gold in the background and in details, clear massing of large areas of color, and a linear quality that is Byzantine at root.

The sitting room of this suite, between Hearst's and the North Gothic Bedroom, is visually one of the densest rooms in the house. Under a heavily restored ceiling of unknown origin, the room is filled with examples of Catholic iconography. Statues and paintings of saints, the Holy Family, prophets, Christ, and a cross give the room an intensely religious feeling. There are nine statues of saints in the room, five of which are of St. Barbara, who, among other things, was the patron saint of architects. Perhaps Hearst knew his enterprise on the Enchanted Hill needed all the help it could get from whatever quarter.

Two of the more popular suites of rooms in the Main Building are the Doge's and the Celestial suites. The most ornate of the large suites is the Doge's Suite. A doge was the elected chief magistrate of the former republics of Venice and Genoa, and the suite probably takes its name from the balcony outside the sitting room, whose

One of a pair of 19th-century Chinese rose quartz statuette lamps in the North Gothic Bedroom.

Opposite: One of San Simeon's smallest, yet certainly most important, paintings is an early 14th-century Madonna and Child by the Sienese painter, Duccio di Buoninsegna, or a very close disciple, possibly Segna di Bonaventura.

Right: The intensity of Hearst's medieval taste is nowhere more pronounced than in his own third-floor Gothic Suite. An old and primitive ceiling—probably from England—sets the mood for a chapel-like theme highlighted by a display of 15th- and 16th-century sculptures of saints and prophets. Two very early pieces of furniture are seen against the side walls: to the left is a flamboyant Gothic chest with allover gilt tracery and, opposite, a late 15th-century French cupboard. At the back wall is a bulky yet richly carved French Gothic mantel. Above: The dominating feature in the North Gothic Bedroom is a rare 15th-century ceiling from Castle Marchino in Cordova, Spain, from which hangs a Florentine silvered bronze lamp. The room contains a collection of early Italian Renaissance pictures. The walnut beds are 1920s reproductions of a 17th-century original; between them an Italian Renaissance chest of drawers supports a pair of Chinese rose quartz statuette lamps.

Venetian balustrade and quatrefoil arches are similar to ones seen on the Doge's Palace in Venice and throughout that city. The sitting room is an experience in opulence. The painted ceiling is one of the more spectacular ceilings in Casa Grande and one of the few that is not in the Spanish-Moorish style. The large painted Annunciation in the middle of it was executed by a student of the Dutch painter Wtewael in the late 16th or early 17th century. Fredericksen wrote, "It is one of the rare ceiling panels from the Netherlands . . . it is such

a curiosity that it deserves special attention."[28] The 16th-century Italian fireplace surmounted by a tondo, framed with a wreath by Giovanni della Robbia (c.1469–c.1529), is a tour de force that effectively competes with the ceiling for attention.

There are also three 16th-century paintings in the room, one of which was once attributed to Jacopo Tintoretto (1518–1594). Fredericksen attributes it to the school of that Venetian master; it contains little of the impetuosity, dramatic contrasts of light and color, or

*A late 15th-century stucco
relief in the style of the Florentine
sculptor Antonio Rossellino, in the
east alcove of the Gothic Study.*

Above left: The Della Robbia Room, above the Doge's Suite, contains a small collection of terra cottas by the Florentine sculptors Andrea and Giovanni della Robbia, as well as this "St. Joseph and the Christ Child" by the workshop of Santi and Benedetto Buglioni, who were contemporaries of the della Robbia family. Below left: A crisply modeled wreath by Giovanni della Robbia encircles a terra-cotta tondo by another artist, who remains unidentified. A pair of iron and bronze candelabra join with the relief in forming an overmantel decoration for the Doge's Sitting Room.

vehemence that are so typical of Tintoretto. Hearst acquired the painting in 1935.

The suite is furnished predominantly with Italian pieces, and is one of the most thematically consistent on the hill and certainly the most luxurious.

Above Hearst's suite of rooms at the very top of Casa Grande is the Celestial Suite. In what might be an apocryphal story, Hearst, one day on an inspection tour with Morgan, was standing on the roof and became so enchanted by the 360-degree view that he said it would be an ideal location for living quarters. Morgan reminded him where they were and that in order to build such a suite of rooms they would have to raise the roof and the completed towers. Never one to let such minutiae stand in his way, Hearst gave the order and the work was initiated and finally completed in 1932.

The suite is hardly distinguished architecturally, suffering perhaps from being so small and so obviously an afterthought. The ceilings, which were made on the site, are overly florid and the decorative panels too large for rooms that size.

The sitting room is dominated by a crudely carved 12th-century French mantel frame around the hearth of the fireplace and three 19th-century French paintings. Two of them, "Bonaparte in Cairo" and "Bonaparte Before the Sphinx," are by Jean-Léon Gérôme (1824–1904), and the third, "Rest on the Flight into Egypt," is by Luc-Olivier Merson (1846–1920); purchased in 1894, the last-named is the earliest of Hearst's purchases on the hill. Both Gérôme and Merson were among a group of French academic salon painters who produced large amounts of skillfully done and overly sentimental paintings. Very popular with visiting Americans at the turn of the century, they have since fallen in critical esteem.

Hearst's participation in the work on the new wing was limited to one and a half years following the war. Certainly he was not as actively involved as he had been before construction stopped. Whether he personally supervised the installation of the furnishings and art objects is open to speculation. He probably selected the items to be included but did not specify where they were to be placed. The

The North Celestial Bedroom, within the north tower of Casa Grande, contains a 16th-century St. John the Baptist and Florentine bed; a 17th-century Italian inlaid walnut chest of drawers; and draperies, window screens, and a plaster of Paris ceiling made in the 1930s.

Opposite: Among the new wing's more attractive rugs is a silk weaving from Kashan, in front of which is the headboard of a Basque bed, a primitive and unique piece of furniture. Below: Detail of the oldest, and possibly most notable, Persian carpet in the collection, the new wing's 18th-century silk Tabriz with an allover decoration of Farsi inscriptions.

Two of the best-preserved paintings in the new wing are the oil-on-panel portraits of Aysma van Lauta and her husband John William Ripperda, dated 1597 and 1609, respectively, attributed to the Flemish painter Frans Pourbus the Younger.

A superb 19th-century Chinese porcelain vase-lamp from the Marion Davies collection. Miniature vase motifs decorate the sides of the piece in an unusual design.

rooms do not have the visual density that was so Hearstian or the powerful and knowing touch that Morgan gave to her previous work.

There is a consistency both in the architecture and in how the pieces are displayed that is not apparent elsewhere. It is, however, a rather bland consistency. The new wing lacks the episodic and dramatic thematic shifts that occur from floor to floor and suite to suite in the prewar work. All of the ceilings, original and new, are Spanish or Spanish-Moorish; the floors of the rooms are terra-cotta tile covered with Oriental rugs, while the art objects are predominantly Italian and Spanish.

The most noteworthy rooms are on the fourth floor. An unsubstantiated rumor has it that Hearst was considering moving into a suite on that floor called the West Tower. The study in that apartment, now called Center Room, while hardly as grand or well made, is reminiscent of the Gothic Study. The main decorative feature is a series of cast-concrete pointed arches painted with scenes of fairy tales by Camille Solon in 1947. Adjacent to the study, in the East Tower, is what may be the oldest ceiling in Casa Grande, a geometrical Moorish dome said to be from the 12th century.

The new wing houses some of the finest rugs on the hill, among which is an exceptional Tabriz hanging in the West Tower on the same floor. The first examples of woven rugs appearing in Persia that can be dated are from Tabriz and its environs. The Tabriz weavers were, from the beginning, profoundly influenced by miniaturists and manuscript illuminators from the Persian court library. The Persian weavers, by using thousands of minuscule knots, much more finely woven than those of Turkish rugs, were able to create incredibly intricate curvilinear forms. The West Tower Tabriz is a superb example of this type of rug. It is a silk-pile rug of complex design. There are also a number of inscriptions woven into the design, among which is the date, 1782, and the name Ali Akbar (presumably the weaver).

The paintings at San Simeon are mainly 14th- and 15th-century Italian; there are some 16th- and 17th-century works as well. In all, there are somewhat over 50 Italian paintings in the collection. The next largest group comprises around 20 Spanish paintings from the 15th and 16th centuries, and a handful each of Dutch, Flemish, German, and French works.

Although the collection contains some secular portraits, the majority of the paintings are religious in theme. Hearst acquired the greater part through the New York auction galleries and some individual dealers. Twenty-five of his Italian paintings were purchased at the famous auctions of the collection of the Milanese Achilito Chiesa, held at The American Art Association Galleries on April 16, 1926, and November 22–23, 1927. It was at that sale that he picked up one of the best paintings in the collection, a 15th-century Madonna and Child by an unknown Umbrian painter which hangs in the new wing.

Other fine paintings in the collection include the "Portrait of a Woman" by the Venetian Giulio Campi (c. 1502–1572), which is in Room 1 on the third floor of the new wing (from the Holford collection, London, which was sold in 1927; Hearst bought it in 1929), and the exceptional "Madonna and Child with Two Angels" by Adriaen Ysenbrandt, a Flemish painter (active c. 1510–1551), which hangs in Casa del Mar. Of this painting Fredericksen wrote, "the Hearst panel is one of his largest and most impressive pictures in America."[29]

The list of first-rate paintings of museum quality also includes the "Assumption of the Virgin with St. James," by the 17th-century Spanish painter Claudio Coello, and the "Portrait of Archduke Ferdinand of Austria," attributed to Christoph Amberger, a German who was active in the 16th century.

The collection at San Simeon is not in the same class as such others as the Norton Simon, Baron von Thyssen, or Frick collections. Hearst bought much without seeming focus. Had he been less ambitious, less compulsive, he might have been far more profound in his selections, less likely to have purchased so much that was second-rate. It is hard to reconcile the extremes of quality among the paintings. But then the collection is probably fairly representative of the contradictions that characterize the man himself.

Opposite: The 16th-century painting, "Madonna and Child with Two Angels" by the Flemish painter Adriaen Ysenbrandt, hangs in Casa del Mar.

*"Portrait of Archduke Ferdinand of Austria," attributed
to the 16th-century German painter Christoph Amberger.*

"Portrait of a Woman" by Giulio Campi, an early 16th-century painting said to represent Isabella d'Este, was acquired by Hearst in 1929, two years after the sale of the Holford collection, London, of which the painting had been a part since the middle of the 19th century.

SAN SIMEON: GROUNDS AND POOLS

EVEN APART FROM what is built there, La Cuesta Encantada has about it the sense of being a very special place. The notion of the special character of a place and the ability of someone to sense, or read, it is one that has been around since people started making decisions about where to settle. It is found in cultures as disparate as those of the American Indians of the Southwest, the ancient Greeks, and the Japanese.

Throughout history, survival has depended upon the ability to "read" a place before making a decision to settle. Survival was believed to be dependent not only upon the place's ability to provide food and water, but upon the presence of forces beyond people's control—local demons and minor gods who might be inhabiting the particular site. The ancient Greeks, for instance, refined this primitive notion of the uniqueness of a place into a mathematical and metaphysical system by which men and gods could establish and maintain a mutually compatible relationship. Since places of habitation subsume all aspects of life, a special social as well as aesthetic unity could be achieved by a correct reading of place.

This is not to suggest that demons inhabit the Enchanted Hill, rather that Hearst not only loved this piece of geography, but through his intimacy with it, was also able to read the bare hill and surrounding landscape before he decided to build. His and Julia Morgan's understanding of the unique and signal elements of the site, steeped

Opposite: Late afternoon view from the Neptune Terrace toward the Santa Lucia mountains. A temple façade, composed of granite columns and marble work from Italy, stands on the west side of the Neptune Pool.

161

in their profound feelings for the place and in their own imaginations, seems to have produced that singular sense of being right, of belonging, that the complex has.

The buildings and grounds have about them the virtue of being an integral and harmonious part of the landscape even though considerable construction altered, at one time or another, the original contours and character of the top of the hill. The successful relationships among buildings, grounds, and countryside speak eloquently of the understanding and appreciation that Morgan and Hearst had for the site, which they carefully altered and crafted so that the transition from the wild and natural bottom of the hill to the manicured top could be made effortlessly and gradually.

Guests of Hearst who visited San Simeon could not help but be even more amazed than the visitor is today. In a private train leased from Southern Pacific, guests would frequently depart from Los Angeles Friday morning and arrive that night in San Luis Obispo, where they were met by a caravan of cars. Driving up the coast, the illuminated buildings and grounds would slowly appear, magically rising out of the darkness and desolation miles away, an improbably impressive, surely evocative occasion in the wilderness: a lighted mountaintop.

If the journey to and up the hill was enchanting by night, by day it was also extraordinary. Viewed from the south, the broad rolling Pacific on the left would, by turn of season or hour, be blue, fog enshrouded, or a misted metallic gray. Ahead, the gentle, broken plain of land, yellow in summer, gradually began to fold into the round and increasingly higher hills that rose to peaks against the sky. And in the distance, small on top of one of the hills, could be seen the ordered pinnacles of Casa Grande, a toy set under a vast space.

The far view enables the visitor to grasp the total environment at first glance: the hilltop with its tiny encrustation of buildings, its relationship to the surrounding higher peaks, and, in turn, their relationship with the sea, the tableland of rolling coast, and the dome of sky. The profound unity of place is made clear as the significant elements of the landscape are juxtaposed harmoniously with each other and with the shaped hilltop. But this total apprehension of the environment is lost as soon as one enters the five-mile-long approach road at the ranch gate and is plunged into a procession of unfolding and changing views and perspectives.

The approach road was designed to do more than just tie Camp Hill to the coast and village of San Simeon; the approach is one of the most dynamic yet subtle progressions toward a work of architecture that exists, rivaling easily the drive to Frank Lloyd Wright's Taliesin West. On the San Simeon road one experiences a visual and sensual series of progressions: an intimate, tightly defined glade, followed by

A marvel of 1920s engineering, the approach drive hugs canyon edges in its 1,600-foot ascent, passing through the former zoo compound and affording sweeping views of mountains and coastline at every turn.

Left: The five-mile approach drive makes its way in and out of small ravines and canyons up the Enchanted Hill, with Casa Grande hidden from view one moment, then suddenly reappearing, each time larger and more visible. Opposite: San Simeon's modern-day zebra herd moves along the flank of a hill.

Left: At the end of the five-mile drive, a flight of stairs leads up to Casa Grande from a cul de sac at the south side of the hill.

an open view of ocean through a framing foreground of trees; the smell of eucalyptus in a deep glen, and cattle across a brilliantly sunlit hillside; and all the while glimpses of the buildings and grounds from below at different angles revealing further clues about the relationship and dynamic of the buildings and the environment. The continuous series of images and impressions not only reveals the harmony between the built and natural; it further tantalizes, producing a state of anticipation and tension that heightens expectations and perceptions and prepares one, as well, for the experience of arrival.

It becomes abundantly clear on the ride up to the top, that not only are the buildings graciously adapted to the contours of the hill, but also that the scale of the buildings—their size in relation to the surrounding country—is also appropriate. They fit. This fit, furthermore, captures the sense of place and enhances it, endowing it with a quality that goes beyond the imposition of an aesthetic order. The buildings complete the hill; they appear as inexorable as a delta, more than the sum of building and site.

Having finally arrived at the top of the hill after a singularly demanding drive, guests had to have been awed, if not by the beauty of the place then by the sheer size, ambitiousness, and awareness of the fact that they had been driving on Hearst land for almost an hour before reaching the top.

That road to the top of the hill, with signs warning motorists "Animals Have the Right of Way," also wove through 2,000 fenced acres of what was once the largest private zoo in the country, if not the world. For those unimpressed by the subtlety of the drive, the sight of the animals, many roving loose, provided entertainment, wonder, and, at times, annoyance. If an animal chose to lie on the warm road in the waning light, an approaching vehicle had nothing to do but wait until the animal roused itself and moved along. Hearst, an impassioned opponent of vivisection, would tolerate no pain or annoyance to be visited upon his animals, from his hand or that of others.

The zoo at one time contained 30 species of carnivores, including tigers, and an elephant named Marianne as well as 70 species of free-roaming grazing animals. The road ran past elaborate bear pits, lion pens, monkey houses, and other assorted shelters for the ani-

Overleaf: Part of the flourishing herd of zebras that graze in the foothills below Casa Grande.

Orchard Hill's zoo compound formerly housed carnivorous animals such as bears and lions, but the majority of Hearst's animals were grazing species that roamed freely over a 2,000-acre compound farther down the hill. Photograph Taylor Coffman.

mals, which were all rebuilt and enlarged after a particularly painful December in 1932, when Hearst lost 11 of his best animals to heavy storms, and wrote to Miss Morgan, "If we are going to lose $10,000 worth of animals a winter . . . and we may lose more than that . . . we can well afford to put up more shelters and the kind which will protect the animals and keep them warm as well as dry." He went on to describe exactly what he wanted and then closed the letter with a detail that underscores his gentle sentiment toward animals: "I think that it would be well to have in connection with two or three of these shelters a room with a fireplace where sick animals could be taken and attended to."[30]

The entire complex is a highly individual and elegant composition made up of a number of parts that expressively describe how Hearst and Morgan strove to create a self-contained world, composed for the most part of discrete environmental episodes. The landscaping—the paths, terraces, gardens, and pool—is as carefully and artfully contrived and built as any part of the buildings. The informality of some of the paths, the free (but careful) positioning of trees, the mixture of clay urns with formal statuary, and the contrast of natural foliage with plants and shrubs whose growth is more rigid demonstrates that Julia Morgan, through the efforts of the gardening staff, was attempting to create the hill's own sense of place.

A narrow, balustraded terrace, broken by occasional flights of stairs to the driveway below, runs from the Neptune Pool to the indoor swimming pool—a distance of about 200 yards. Along its north edge stand a number of the huge Italian cypresses that Hearst transported from Paso Robles, 30 miles away.

Near Casa del Monte.

On the Neptune Terrace.

In front of Casa Grande.

In the main gardens.

In the main gardens.

Below Casa del Sol.

Marble lampposts, all fitted with electric lights, decorated the grounds of the estate. Many were sculpted of Carrara marble by the Brothers Romanelli, Florence.

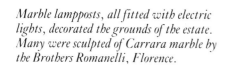

On the Main Terrace.

On the Esplanade.

In the fishpond, Main Terrace.

Opposite and right: Cast-stone lampposts near the Neptune Pool.

With a minimum of materials she was able to create a number of microworlds in close proximity to one another. On the Esplanade, for example, outside House C and House B, one is scarcely aware of the presence of Casa Grande and the Main Terrace, which together make a curiously powerful urban statement set in the surrounding wilderness. Instead, one is as sheltered in that tight space and the contrasting light and shade as one would be in a rural Mediterranean patio. It is a masterwork of stagecraft.

The lighting scheme for the hill was also thoughtfully designed, outlined in typically Hearstian detail in a letter to Julia Morgan. As in all his other communiqués, he was quite sure about what he wanted, and demonstrated a mastery of the problems of theatrical illumination acquired no doubt from his years of movie making. He specified not only the number of fixtures necessary for the desired effect, but also designed the actual fixtures for the cascade and pool terraces: "The very best thing to do is to put the caryatids that you are going to make into a pergola and make them carry lamps on their heads." [31]

It is easy to appreciate the unlikelihood of the place and at once the range of minds and talents that organized this assemblage of structures, terraces, sculptural items, plant beds, steps, and subtle axial relationships and views. What is not so easy to appreciate, because the results all seem so natural, is the effort, the physical work that was necessary to make the place. The creation of the grounds and adjacent hillside planting was as impressive a task as the construction of the buildings. As the guests strolled in the gardens, went swimming, played tennis, picnicked, or rode horseback through the espaliered-tree-lined, mile-long pergola—"the longest pergola in captivity"[32]—almost all of the landscaping they passed through or saw had been made and remade. The North Terrace, for instance, is built over an existing flight of stairs and smaller landings, which, sometime in the late 1920s, having been found unsatisfactory in relation to other changes or proposals, was entirely covered by new construction.

Work on the grounds began the same year construction started, 1920. Hearst brought his close boyhood friend, Orrin Peck, down from San Francisco to design the gardens for him. Peck, an established portrait painter, found himself in financial difficulties and so welcomed the opportunity to do some design work for his friend. He worked at the hill until early in 1921, when, while visiting a friend in

Opposite above and below: Surrounding Orchard Hill, below the Neptune Pool, in a serpentine course of more than a mile is a concrete-columned pergola, once espaliered with fruit-bearing trees and covered with grapevines.

Los Angeles, he died suddenly of a heart attack. That year Hearst met Nigel Keep, an Englishman who would remain with him as employee and friend for some 30 years. Keep, who was working in a nursery in Niles, California, cautioned Hearst, who was buying some fruit trees, that the trees were of poor quality and that he should save his money. So unique was it for Hearst to receive honest advice from anybody who had something to sell him that he immediately made Keep an offer that turned out to be—like everything else on the ranch—more than just a job; it became Keep's life's work.

Over the years, Keep and a crew upwards of 20 groundsmen transformed the rocky knob covered only with sparse oaks, manzanita, greasewood, and other semidesert shrubs, into an amazement of horticulture. The entire southwest slope of the hill was planted with lemon and orange trees. In 1930, some 6,000 pine trees were put in on an adjacent hill, entirely transforming a view Hearst did not like by obscuring the 1,250,000-gallon reservoir that provided the water for the grounds. On other adjacent tops, slopes, and ridges reaching down to the coast, it is estimated that between 70,000 and 100,000 trees—eucalyptus, cedar, and acacia—were planted under Keep's supervision. The topsoil hauled up from below to provide the growing medium was enough to cover over 50 acres, five feet deep.

The cypress trees bordering the North Terrace were mature 30-foot-tall specimens when they were taken out of the ground in Paso Robles, boxed, and then trucked 30 miles over the mountains to the site. Hearst, who could not bear having trees cut down unnecessarily, had any oak endangered by the construction boxed and moved. Boxing and moving a tree of mature size was a major construction project. A trench would be dug around the tree at the drip line to a depth of about eight or ten feet; into this trench concrete would be poured and allowed to cure. A ramp would then be dug down to the bottom of the concrete wall and shores put in as the dirt was picked and shoveled out by miners hired specially to do this work (the regular construction workers refused). The box containing the tree, roots, and dirt would then be jacked up, log rollers slipped under it, and then be rolled up the ramp to its new position on the site. One oak tree, a 150-year-old specimen, which weighed over 100 tons with box and soil, took six months to move 25 feet when it was found to be in the way of construction of the service wing.

As each part or side of the house was completed, the immediate area was landscaped, so that some progress was constantly being made at turning the construction site into a more agreeable place. The flowers in the gardens that Hearst loved, guests admired, and no one was allowed to pick, were propagated in three of five greenhouses on the site (the remaining two were for the display of begonias). Some 500,000 to 700,000 annuals were propagated each year for cyclical and seasonal display, so that at all times the gardens were abundant with new blossoms. Often, desiring some special effect that could not be achieved with what was on hand, Hearst would have massive quantities of flowers trucked in—lilies at Easter, for example; the groundsmen would put them in the beds overnight for the astonishment of all in the morning.

The gardens, like everything else Hearst was interested in, came under his critical scrutiny. Arriving from New York for one of his visits before he had permanently moved to the hill, Hearst would note changes made, quality of maintenance, and the colors of flowers, and issue verbal directives to Keep and written letters to Morgan about his concerns: "Mrs. Hearst when she arrived felt the same way that I did about the geranium and lantana borders. They have all gone to pieces, and they were . . . so beautiful as always to excite comment from visitors. Putting in the geraniums is, I think, a mistake. The color scheme is no longer attractive."[33]

The grounds crews worked year-round changing floral displays, replacing azaleas, feeding soil, battling erosion, and tending to the nearly 3,000 rose plants of 84 varieties, some of them today the only remaining examples of a particular variety alive in the country.

The first flowers planted on the hill, around House A, were Hearst's favorite, camellias. To these hedges over the years have been added hedges of star jasmine and azalea, bordering the steps from the Neptune Pool to the Neptune Terrace. The Esplanade connecting the smaller houses was planted in a profusion of varieties, star jasmine and azalea enriched by large rhododendron, fragrant daphne, intensely colored fuchsia, and acanthus. A number of types of decorative citrus add to the color and perfume the air as one walks past the neat borders of lantana, aralia shrubs, and exquisite flowering maples. There are of course other varieties on the hill, blossoming sequentially throughout most of the year so that for as long as is possible the air is perfumed and the eye delighted.

Late afternoon in the main gardens.

*Left: Dense foliage—a legacy of the English garden—
between Casa Grande's Main Terrace and the Esplanade.
Below: View of the gardens from Casa del Mar toward
the service wing.*

Casa Grande shrouded in fog behind lush gardens.

*"Europa," c. 1920, by German sculptor Fritz Behn,
among the roses in the main gardens.*

Precisely manicured hedges of Japanese and Korean boxwood near Casa del Monte.

*Red and pink rhododendron
frame a copy of Donatello's "David,"
which surmounts a tall marble
fountain below Casa del Sol.*

Keeping the fruit trees alive in spite of field mice and rat attacks was a particularly vexatious job, doubly so since Hearst was vehemently opposed to causing the death of animals. George Loorz, the last of Hearst's superintendents, once wrote Hearst's secretary Willicombe about the problem: ". . . regarding the plague of rodents we are having on the hilltop. The orchard is literally crawling with the animals . . . they are destroying his [Keep's] young plants as fast as he plants them. Perhaps the varmints [which had been removed] were an important factor in destroying field mice." Hearst replied, "O.K., bring on the executioner. I do not think the plague is due to absence of 'varmints.' Every once in a while there is a plague of something or other . . . locusts or grasshoppers or frogs or rats or politicians . . . something to afflict us. It has been so in all recorded time . . . and the politicians are the worst. If we ever get rid of them let us institute a special Passover."[34]

The grounds that the visitor sees today, while similar in layout and containing much of the original plant material, are clearly not as they were in the 1920s and '30s. Obviously, plant materials, subject to the cyclical vagaries of sun, rain, and insect infestation, change and grow with maturity and decay as well. But enough of the original trees, hedges, and flowers do exist so that the gardens not only reflect fairly accurately the original but, being more mature, are, in fact, more magnificent today than they were when Hearst strolled the grounds.

Construction of the largest nonresidential building on the hill—an extensive athletic facility—was begun in late 1926 or early 1927. It was located northeast of the Main Building. The complex was to provide facilities for the more seriously athletic guests. Some elements of the original proposal were not realized, mainly the fully equipped gymnasium, but the outdoor lighted tennis courts, the indoor swimming pool and dressing rooms were completed. The pool, like everything else on the hill, was ambitious and outsized. While not particularly distinguished architecturally, it is an impressive visual experience. The room's light and water are suffused by the deep blue color of the Venetian tile, making it appear that one is submerged in an enormous, shimmering aquarium.

There was a good deal of muted contention in the letters between Hearst and Morgan over delays in completing the pool on time. He was growing very impatient indeed with the progress, especially since it was being impeded by the poor work habits and continual changes demanded by the designer in Morgan's employ, Camille Solon. Solon, who was designing the tile work, and who painted the arches of the Gothic Suite and the sitting room of the fourth floor of the new wing, would leave his work undone for weeks at a time. As diplomatically as he could, and he usually behaved that way with Morgan, Hearst asked in a letter if she could find need for Solon in

San Francisco. Morgan, with her usual aplomb, ignored the request. She explained the matter to Solon, put more men on the job, and was able to report to Hearst that progress was being made.

John Pellegrini, a tile contractor of San Francisco, who had done work on the hill before, was hired to get the work going on schedule. Working from Solon's designs, which Thaddeus Joy probably modified, Pellegrini's men would glue the tile to panels on which the designs had been drawn. The panels would then be shipped from San Francisco to San Simeon where they would be mortared in place. The pool was further decorated by statuary, reproductions of Greek and Roman classical works whose emplacement seems an afterthought. The marble lamp standards, however, with their alabaster globes, are clearly basic to the design scheme. The room is much more impressive at night than during the day, since, when it is lit, the exterior disappears and the soft, pale orange light reflecting in the windows and the blue water transforms the room into a special kind of pleasure dome.

Massive reinforced concrete beams, a profusion of glass tiles from Murano, Italy, marble reproductions of classical statues, and amber lighting from alabaster lampshades produce a bewitching effect in the indoor swimming pool.

Overleaf
Left: One of eight Carrara marble sculptures commissioned of Carlo Freter of Pietrasanta, Italy, expressly for the indoor swimming pool. All are reproductions of famous classical works; here, "Diana and the Deer" occupies an alcove resplendent with Italian glass tile, some with surfaces of gold. Marble lamp standards by the Brothers Romanelli of Florence provide the sole source of light at night for the grotto-like room. *Right:* A diving balcony, decorated with gilt tile work, is cantilevered over the main body of the indoor swimming pool. A 17th-century Italian statue, "Abundantia," stands at the back of a shallower wading alcove.

Impressive as the indoor swimming pool is, it pales by comparison to the Elysian beauty of the Neptune Pool. The formal geometry of the pool, the colonnades, and the temple façade set against the near and far views of trees and mountains, are as evocative of the Old World as any setting on the hill, recalling the romantic fantasies of Maxfield Parrish and images of Hadrian's Villa outside Rome. The clear blue-green color of the water is not the result of colored tile used to face the pool but rather the effect of daylight's refraction by the water. The pool itself, and the surrounding apron, are made of contrasting white and dark-green Vermont marble.

The disposition of the forms within the pool's overall composition of walls, terraces, and stairs was the result of a long, frustrating, and expensive process. The pool was subject to considerable change. The first pool was completely torn out and rebuilt. Thought too small, it was substantially enlarged before the present design was found satisfactory. As the landscape and terraces changed in relation to the growth of the buildings or a previous gesture was corrected, the terraces around the pool and the pool itself had also to be altered to remain in harmonious balance and respond to the new sets of relationships.

The existing temple façade was threatened with alterations after the pool took its present shape because Hearst wanted to build a bathhouse on its site. Morgan, instead, discreetly tucked the dressing rooms under the Neptune Terrace (now called the Tea Terrace), sparing the façade, herself, and the workmen another round of demolition and construction. The temple façade was bought as one piece; although the columns, the entablature, and the pediment of the façade date from different times, all come from Italy. The colonnades on the north and south ends of the pool, however, are new. The top balustrade and cornice were made in the shops on the site out of cast stone.

Most of the figures around the pool and in it were carved by the French sculptor, Charles Cassou, who worked in Paris during the 1920s and '30s. The large Birth of Venus groups were ordered by Hearst in January 1927. For the large central niche opposite the temple façade, Cassou had also carved a large Neptune Triumphant, complete with horses straining through turbulent foamy seas, thematically reminiscent of the Trevi fountain in Rome. For some reason, this group was never installed. Of all the statuary Hearst bought or

View of the Neptune Pool and temple façade through one of the colonnades.

Below: View through the Neptune Pool's south colonnade toward the Pacific. Opposite: Between the Neptune Pool and Terrace stand some of the Italian cypresses that were brought to the hill as mature trees.

Dreamlike views of the Neptune Pool enveloped in mist.

Opposite: Romantic view from the Neptune Terrace. Left: A bathhouse with 17 dressing rooms for the Neptune Pool serves as a foundation for the Neptune Terrace. Below: A parade of cast-stone termini—1930s copies of a Graeco-Roman boundary marker in the Hearst collection—flank the steps from the Neptune Pool to its bathhouse above.

commissioned, Cassou's are the most affected and lifeless, the kind of thing found in world's fairs or movie lobbies at that time. They are out of place and seem afterthoughts since they do not contribute to heightening the existing tensions of the overall composition nor do they serve to focus attention. Perhaps the Neptune Triumphant would have contributed to the overall composition.

The pool is not built entirely into the ground. The shallow south end is built upon a large terrace, projecting out and over the natural contours and supported on columns, while the deep end is excavated into the hill. The large settling pools, filtering tanks, and water heating system were built in the space below the terrace. Only the filtering system is operating today; and the 345,000 gallons of water are as clear as they were when Hearst used the pool.

The Neptune Pool and its terrace fit effortlessly into the freely interpreted Italianate composition of terraces and stairs that cascades down the hill from the Main Terrace. The vast terraces, rivers of stairs, and major plant areas required a reshaping of the hilltop that would retain a sense of deliberate design gestures without the destruction of the hill's basic characteristics. Most of the terraces on the west and north sides of the hill are built well up and out in the air over natural contours or earlier terraces and stairs in order to gain the visual space necessary to create the proper relationships among the various levels. The terraces and grounds are a major work of landscape art, every bit as important and well executed as the buildings

Opposite: Romantic view from the Neptune Terrace. Left: A bathhouse with 17 dressing rooms for the Neptune Pool serves as a foundation for the Neptune Terrace. Below: A parade of cast-stone termini—1930s copies of a Graeco-Roman boundary marker in the Hearst collection—flank the steps from the Neptune Pool to its bathhouse above.

commissioned, Cassou's are the most affected and lifeless, the kind of thing found in world's fairs or movie lobbies at that time. They are out of place and seem afterthoughts since they do not contribute to heightening the existing tensions of the overall composition nor do they serve to focus attention. Perhaps the Neptune Triumphant would have contributed to the overall composition.

The pool is not built entirely into the ground. The shallow south end is built upon a large terrace, projecting out and over the natural contours and supported on columns, while the deep end is excavated into the hill. The large settling pools, filtering tanks, and water heating system were built in the space below the terrace. Only the filtering system is operating today; and the 345,000 gallons of water are as clear as they were when Hearst used the pool.

The Neptune Pool and its terrace fit effortlessly into the freely interpreted Italianate composition of terraces and stairs that cascades down the hill from the Main Terrace. The vast terraces, rivers of stairs, and major plant areas required a reshaping of the hilltop that would retain a sense of deliberate design gestures without the destruction of the hill's basic characteristics. Most of the terraces on the west and north sides of the hill are built well up and out in the air over natural contours or earlier terraces and stairs in order to gain the visual space necessary to create the proper relationships among the various levels. The terraces and grounds are a major work of landscape art, every bit as important and well executed as the buildings

Opposite above: Two of four sculptures of Nymphs and Swans made for the Neptune Pool by Charles Cassou. Opposite below: View of the Neptune Pool and Terrace, with Casa Grande's towers and new wing in the background. Above: The "Birth of Venus," by Cassou, occupies an alcove on the east side of the Neptune Pool.

Overleaf: Curving staircases lead from Casa del Sol to the spacious, palm-lined terrace from which Orchard Hill, the lower Hearst ranch, and miles of rocky coastline can be seen.

Left: A panorama of mountain scenery lies to the north in this view from the Main Terrace across the small Mountain Earring Terrace, so named for the semicircular white marble benches that frame a Venetian "Floreale" wellhead. Above: At the west end of the South Terrace is a Renaissance wellhead bought by Hearst in Verona, Italy, in the 1890s, which for many years graced the courtyard of his mother's estate near Pleasanton. Below: Venetian "Floreale" wellhead.

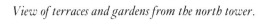
View of terraces and gardens from the north tower.

Ceramic tile pavers used in terraces and walks on the hill.

One of many ceramic tiles manufactured for San Simeon at California Faience, Berkeley, in the 1920s.

Below: Detail of a radiating circular design of terra-cotta and ceramic tile pavement on the South Terrace. Opposite: Pavement inserts of vert antique marble near the Neptune Pool.

themselves; they serve, at the same time, as a showcase for some of the important original sculptures and reproductions in the collection.

The oldest piece in Hearst's collection is found south of the Main Terrace along the Esplanade. Carved in a very dark igneous stone is the lion-headed Egyptian goddess Sekhmet. Attributed by some to the 18th Dynasty, the figures could be almost 3,500 years old.

Below House C on its circular terrace is a bronze copy of the famous "David" by the 15th-century Florentine sculptor, Donatello. The fountain and the "David" function perfectly, giving focus to the space before House C and creating an object in the middle distance behind which the elegant Italianate loggia of the house is seen from C Terrace.

There are two other bronzes, on C Terrace, both 20th-century copies. One is an excellent copy by Umberto Marcellini of a Nike figure—the Greek goddess of victory—gazing into a mirror. The other is a copy of an ancient Roman marble in the Vatican, of Discobolus, a discus thrower, which is itself a copy of a Greek original.

Both of these figures, left where found when the state acquired the property, are poorly placed against the balustrade of the terrace, opposite each other. Their location prevents the visitor from walking around them. They would be more effective in a location of greater prominence, one where they could not only be seen properly, but where they could also provide meaning to a space—the end of a vista or perhaps at either end of the Neptune Terrace, where the green patina of the naturalistic figures would provide a suitable transition from the classical formality of the Neptune Pool area to the bosky romanticism of the Esplanade.

Perhaps the best outdoor sculpture on the hill is the "Galatea," facing the front of the Main Building across the fishpond. It was carved by Leopoldo Ansiglioni of Rome in the 1880s and is a stunning example of the stone cutter's art. As the languid Galatea reclines on a dolphin, her brooding face and sensual body contrast with her vigorously sculpted, swirling hair, the dolphin's thrashing tail, and the cloth covering her left leg. These dynamically carved elements effectively suggest the surf through which the dolphin carries her. The placement of this piece is evidence that both Hearst and Morgan thought it exceptional.

The rest of the statuary is placed as though Morgan and Hearst wanted to surprise the stroller. One comes upon a piece around a bush or set casually by a path. Most of them are of no great artistic moment, but delightful garden pieces used in a pleasant and traditional way.

The grounds at San Simeon are not as large as the more famous Italian Renaissance gardens such as those of the Villa d'Este outside Rome or the Boboli gardens in Florence, but they make use of all the

Below: Adolph Daumiller's bronze figure, "The First Rose," stands on a boldly sculptured fountain on the west side of Casa del Mar. Opposite: "David" faces westward toward Orchard Hill and the Pacific from his fountain perch below Casa del Sol. It is not known when or by whom this copy of Donatello's famous bronze was made.

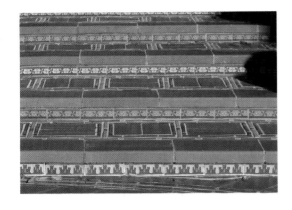

Many of the exterior stairways are decorated with risers of ceramic tile, made by California Faience, Berkeley, from designs of Spanish derivation submitted by Julia Morgan. Below: Rare golden azaleas and purple lantana mark the beginning of Azalea Walk, a section of the Esplanade running alongside the new wing.

Above: Art Deco lotus motif at the Sekhmet fountain. Right: Oldest of San Simeon's art works are the four black granite Egyptian sculptures that decorate a fountain along the Esplanade. Each represents the lion-headed deity Sekhmet and dates to around 1500 B.C.

Below and opposite: "Galatea" by Leopoldo Ansiglioni, a late 19th-century Italian sculptor, in the Main Terrace fishpond. The figure reclines on a dolphin, supported by a heavy gray marble base on a serpentine plinth.

individual Renaissance elements—sculpture, fountains, arbors, water ponds, birds, exotic animals, and geometric design, but one less rigid than that of the typical Renaissance garden. The grounds also share another important characteristic with the Renaissance garden: a cinematographic sense.

Because of San Simeon's intersecting axial paths, as in the Renaissance garden, and curving major paths, the visitor is constantly made aware of something else to come as the vista shifts. A piece of sculpture, a bright area seen from a shaded place, a broad view glimpsed from a narrow area, all conspire to encourage movement and the continuous experience of the grounds from an ever-changing set of visual relationships. The visitor becomes not just a passive viewer but an active protagonist in the environmental spectacle.

Above: A Carrara marble Cupid rides a dolphin along a South Terrace balustrade. Below: The carved surface of an ancient Roman sarcophagus and the delicacy of a sculpture of the Three Graces show to advantage in diffused garden light. Right: "Mars and Cupid," by Umberto Marcellini, 1929, among the hydrangeas, rhododendron, and native live oaks.

Above: High-relief carving on the front of a Roman sarcophagus represents a battle between Achilles and the Queen of the Amazons. Opposite above: Resting on a bulky Roman sarcophagus is a sepulchral monument of marble carved with the portraits of a father, mother, and son. Opposite below: An unusual 16th-century boat-shaped wellhead on the east end of the South Terrace.

A copy of the Venus Anadyomene in the Museo delle Terme, Rome, stands in the gardens between Casa del Monte and Casa del Sol.

Break of day over Arroyo de la Cruz after a rainy April night.

Afterword

SOMETIME BEFORE 10:00 A.M. on August 14, 1951, William Randolph Hearst, 88 years old, died quietly.

After his death it seemed the world had lost a natural force. He was eulogized, damned, but he was remembered as an original who defined much of the time in which he lived. Hearst's enemies—who were legion—have always concluded that the man was void of all virtue. Those who were against him were unable to balance the good he did in his life against what they thought was evil. His concerns about social inequities, economic imbalances, and political corruption, were seen as the acts of a man pandering to potential readers and voters in order to realize his private political ambitions and to fill his pockets.

Hearst was never an evil man; at worst he was a selfish and ruthless person possessed of an enormous ego. He was also a person who appeared wholly self-sufficient and who had an almost cavalier disregard for established convention.

Immediately following Hearst's death, his body was flown to San Francisco where it lay in state inside Grace Episcopal Cathedral. It was the first time he had been inside the church since his mother's funeral. Among those who served as honorary pallbearers were ex-President Herbert Hoover, Governor Earl Warren of California, General Douglas MacArthur, Bernard Baruch, and Louis B. Mayer.

The funeral cortege and police motorcycle escort moved to Cypress

Lawn Cemetery, a few miles south of San Francisco, where he was entombed in the Hearst mausoleum alongside George Hearst and Phoebe Apperson Hearst.

Marion Davies, out of deference to the feelings of the family, did not attend the funeral or the church services.

The privilege of burying and honoring Hearst fell to his widow, Millicent, who after years of estrangement and separation still proudly carried his name in spite of the obvious emotional pain they had caused each other.

Julia Morgan was 79 years old when Hearst died. That same year, 1951, after suffering a series of strokes, she was placed in the care of a nurse in her home in Oakland, never fully recovering. She died in San Francisco at the age of 85 in 1957. With her reserve about publicity, Morgan's reputation went into a brief eclipse. In a story *Life* magazine did on San Simeon in the 1950s her name was not even mentioned. Perhaps it was as she would have wanted it, but journalistically it was a grievous omission, delaying, perhaps, a proper assessment of Morgan's place in 20th-century architecture.

Hearst's sons were named trustees of the three trusts that his will directed to be created. One trust made Millicent Hearst the beneficiary of $6,000,000 in Hearst Corporation preferred stock and $1,500,000 in cash. Another trust for his sons assured them a comfortable yearly return on preferred corporation stock plus 100 shares each of corporation voting stock. A third trust made the University of California, the Los Angeles County Museum of Art, and any other groups or individuals deemed appropriate by a foundation Hearst had set up, the recipients of monies for educational and charitable purposes. His will, 125 pages long, gave instructions for the disposition of his total diminished personal estate of $59,500,000.

One year after Hearst died, the hilltop, some 125 acres, was offered to the state of California by the Hearst Corporation. A resolution was adopted in the state legislature in March 1954 to accept the gift, and the next four years were spent determining the precise terms by which California would take title. Seven years after his death, the Enchanted Hill became the property of the state of California. On June 2, 1958, with all due ceremony, La Cuesta Encantada was opened to the public. On that day a bronze plaque was installed on the Main Terrace before the big house. It reads:

LA CUESTA ENCANTADA
PRESENTED TO THE STATE OF CALIFORNIA
IN 1958 BY THE HEARST CORPORATION,
IN MEMORY OF WILLIAM RANDOLPH
HEARST, WHO CREATED THIS ENCHANTED
HILL, AND OF HIS MOTHER, PHOEBE
APPERSON HEARST, WHO INSPIRED IT.

On the plaque on the top of the hill and another one at the bottom in the Visitors Center, Julia Morgan's name and the recognition of the role she played were thoughtlessly omitted.

From that opening day the hill has been one of the most popular visitors' attractions in California. Excluding San Francisco, Los Angeles, and Disneyland, it draws more visitors a year than any other single location in California. It is the only facility run by the Department of Parks and Recreation that returns significant amounts of money to the general fund. Unfortunately, not all of that money is returned to the facility for needed maintenance and restoration, and the park rangers, in whose effective care the hill was placed, are hampered in their efforts at maintenance. Given the number of yearly visitors, it is a testament to the park rangers' efforts that the place is in as good shape as it is, but signs of wear are seen, and the hill, sorely taxed as it is, is in desperate need of an adequately funded program of continual maintenance, restoration, and museology.

In past years, all of the money generated by the hill was available for use at the site. But more recently, all of the money has gone into the state's general fund and not enough of it returns. For example, in fiscal 1977–78, around 885,000 people paid to visit the hill and generated a total of almost $4,500,000. That amount went into the general fund. It takes about $3,000,000 to pay for just the operating expenses, salaries of the 77 permanent employees, the 114 intermittent employees, the additional 106 seasonal workers, the contract for the buses, and so on. Funds for maintaining the grounds and buildings and for restoration of interiors and art objects must be requested annually by staff and dispensed from the general fund by the governor's office and the legislature.

In 1977–78, out of the $4,500,000 that went into that fund, the Hearst Monument received $450,000 for maintenance and restoration in addition to the $3,000,000 for operating expenses. Fifty thousand dollars of that went for work on the interiors and restoration. Clearly, that kind of money is wholly inadequate. The Hearst Monument is a major museum, and to have its budget ultimately determined by politicians is an act of exquisite folly. The state, excellent as it is in maintaining a magnificent park system, is ill equipped to maintain a museum collection. There is a tremendous need for a qualified curatorial staff to carry out this task with sufficient funds to maintain and restore the buildings, grounds, and works of art, and to expand the body of knowledge about the Hearst Monument.

What Hearst and Morgan created is too important a work to be allowed to fall into even slight disrepair; it would be irresponsible to the future, a disservice to the present, and an insult to the memories of William Randolph Hearst, Julia Morgan, and the craftsmen who so lovingly created this most magical and beautiful place for all to enjoy.

Notes

1 *New York Journal-American*, March 4, 1947.

2 William A. Swanberg, *Citizen Hearst* (New York: Charles Scribner's Sons, 1961).

3 James Creelman, *On the Great Highway* (Boston, 1901).

4 Harriet Rochlin, "Westways Women: Designed by Julia Morgan," *Westways*, vol. 68, no. 3, March 1976.

5 Elinor Richey, *Eminent Women of the West* (Berkeley: Howell-North Books, 1975).

6 Ibid.

7 Flora and Morgan North, typescript of an oral history conducted by Suzanne B. Reiss, 1974–75, for the Julia Morgan Architectural History Project, Regional Oral History Office, The Bancroft Library, University of California, Berkeley.

8 Walter Steilberg, typescript of an oral history conducted by Sally Woodbridge, 1972, for the Julia Morgan Architectural History Project, Regional Oral History Office, The Bancroft Library, University of California, Berkeley.

9 William Randolph Hearst, Jr., to the author.

10 Walter Steilberg, op. cit.

11 William Randolph Hearst, Correspondence, The Bancroft Library, University of California, Berkeley.

12 Ibid.

13 Ibid.

14 Ibid.

15 Ibid.

16 Flora and Morgan North, op. cit.

17 Walter Steilberg, op. cit.

18 William Randolph Hearst, op. cit.

19 Ibid.

20 Ibid.

21 Ibid.

22 Anna Marguerite McCann, *Roman Sarcophagi in The Metropolitan Museum of Art* (New York: The Metropolitan Museum of Art, 1978).

23 Dorothy Wormser Coblentz, typescript of an oral history conducted by Leslie Freudenheim and Elizabeth Sussman, c. 1971, for the Julia Morgan Architectural History Project, Regional Oral History Office, University of California, Berkeley.

24 William Randolph Hearst, Jr., to the author.

25 Edmond D. Coblentz, *W. R. Hearst: A Portrait in His Own Words* (New York: Simon & Schuster, 1952).

26 The lamp came from the Hacienda near Pleasanton; it is not known if William Randolph Hearst or Phoebe Hearst purchased it.

27 William Randolph Hearst, op. cit.

28 Burton B. Fredericksen, *Handbook of the Paintings in the Hearst San Simeon State Historical Monument* (Delphinian Publications, 1977).

29 Ibid.

30 William Randolph Hearst, op. cit.

31 Ibid.

32 Ibid.

33 Ibid.

34 Edmond D. Coblentz, op. cit.

Appendix

Of the many myths that surround the Enchanted Hill, one of the most prevalent and inaccurate is that Hearst spent between $30,000,000 and $50,000,000 on it. Where that figure came from is not known, although it is possible that Hearst himself, in a joking mood or for reasons of ego, started the false rumor.

Among the records and correspondence of Julia Morgan, once held by Morgan and Flora North, her nephew (deceased) and his wife, and now at The California Polytechnic State University, San Luis Obispo, a number of memos deal with the major construction projects at San Simeon with dollar amounts attached. One of the memos was dated July 26, 1945, and was sent to William Murray of the Sunical Land and Livestock Corporation, owners of the Piedra Blanca ranch. It is a breakdown of San Simeon construction expenditures, 1919 to 1942 inclusive. The memo was drawn up by Morgan or someone in her office. There was no other agency or person who would have that information since Morgan's office was in charge of the whole operation—ordered materials, hired workers, supervised construction, paid salaries, bills, even bought food for the workers—and would, therefore, have the only accurate account of what was spent.

Including the work done in San Simeon village (housing and warehouses) the total came to $4,717,000: San Simeon village, $110,000; animal shelters, $40,000; houses A, B, and C, $550,000; Main Building, $2,987,000; tennis courts and Roman plunge, $400,000;

Neptune Pool, $430,000; animal hill, cages and arenas, $35,000; waterline, $25,000; reservoirs, $85,000; sewers, septic tanks, and lighting, $35,000; and temporary construction (workers' quarters and the like), $20,000.

One item not listed is the outdoor work—terraces and landscaping. In a May 21, 1931, letter to Hearst, Morgan wrote, "65 percent of budget money goes into grading, trucks . . . bear and lion pits, rock wall, fences, meals, . . . general camp expense and warehousing" (William Randolph Hearst, Correspondence, The Bancroft Library, University of California, Berkeley). Morgan assigned a proportional amount of the total cost of the grounds expenditure within the project boundary of each of the individual building projects so that she was able to keep track of those costs, a frequent architectural practice. Therefore, all the exterior work, excluding statuary and other built-in architectural elements from the collection, is included in the $4,717,000 figure. Under landscaping would be included the costs associated with hauling and placing of all soil on the hill, tree moving, plant materials, trees, terraces, steps, fountains, and pools. Dividing the $4,717,000 by the total square footage of all the buildings listed yields a cost per square foot of $41.78.

During the 1920s and '30s, construction costs for first-class public buildings such as reinforced concrete, stone-faced university facilities, in California, were running about $6 to $7 per square foot. Given the isolation of San Simeon and the amount of special and exacting work that went into it, such a difference (six to seven times prevailing costs) can only be explained by assuming that the figures included everything: shipping, material costs, labor (laborers received about $1 per day, while skilled artisans such as Jules Suppo made around $1.50 per hour), cabinet work, food and housing for the workers, and so on. That total most probably includes some furnishings: silk wall coverings, drapes, curtains, as well as contemporary furniture such as the easy chairs and couches in the Assembly Room. It would not reflect expenditures for most of the furniture, antiques, or art works, since, according to Taylor Coffman, those items were acquired and delivered to San Simeon through a process in which Morgan's office played a limited role. Coffman, who has totalled the time-of-purchase costs of most of those items, estimates that $1,500,000 to $2,500,000 was spent for furnishings and art work and another $1,000,000 for those items from the collection that were built in.

Absent from these figures is work done after World War II, the completion of the new wing, but that relatively minor portion of the project would not affect the overall costs significantly. The grand total Hearst spent on San Simeon was no more than $7,200,000 to $8,200,000.

The cost of building today what is seen there, excluding the art acquisitions, would be between $50,000,000 and $60,000,000, given present-day costs.

Selected Bibliography

BOOKS

Bonfils, Winifred. *The Life and Personality of Phoebe Apperson Hearst*. San Francisco: J. H. Nash, 1928.

Carson, Oliver, and Ernest S. Bates. *Hearst, Lord of San Simeon*. New York: Viking Press, 1936.

Coblentz, Edmond D. *W. R. Hearst: A Portrait in His Own Words*. New York: Simon & Schuster, 1952.

Davies, Marion. *The Times We Had*. Indianapolis: Bobbs-Merrill, 1975.

Fredericksen, Burton B. *Handbook of the Paintings in the Hearst San Simeon State Historical Monument*. Delphinian Publications, 1977.

Hamilton, Geneva. *Where the Highway Ends*. Cambria: Williams Printing, 1974.

Hearst, William Randolph. *Selections from the Writings and Speeches of William Randolph Hearst*. San Francisco, 1948.

Lewis, Oscar. *Fabulous San Simeon*. San Francisco: California Historical Society, 1958.

Longstreth, Richard W. *Julia Morgan, Architect*. Berkeley: Berkeley Architectural Heritage Association, 1977.

Murray, Ken. *The Golden Days of San Simeon*. Garden City, N. Y.: Doubleday, 1971.

Older, Fremont. *The Life of George Hearst*. Los Angeles: Westernlore, 1966.

Richey, Elinor. *Eminent Women of the West*. Berkeley: Howell-North Books, 1975.

St. Johns, Adela Rogers. *The Honeycomb*. New York: New American Library, 1970.

Swanberg, William A. *Citizen Hearst*. New York: Charles Scribner's Sons, 1961.

Tebbel, John William. *The Life and Good Times of William Randolph Hearst*. New York: Dutton, 1952.

Towner, Wesley. *The Elegant Auctioneers*. New York: Hill & Wang, 1970.

ARTICLES

Boutelle, Sara. "The Long-Distance Dreamer Who Altered the Look of California." *California Monthly*, April 1976.

North, Flora D. "She Built for the Ages." *Kappa Alpha Theta*, Spring 1967.

Rochlin, Harriet. "Westways Women: Designed by Julia Morgan." *Westways*, vol. 68, no. 3, March 1976.

Scharloch, Bernice. "The Legacy of Julia Morgan." *California Living*, August 24, 1975.

"Unique Tour of San Simeon." *Life*, August 26, 1957.

ARCHIVES

The Bancroft Library, University of California, Berkeley:
    Edmond D. Coblentz Papers.

    Papers of Phoebe Apperson Hearst.

    The William Randolph Hearst Collection, Correspondence.

    Julia Morgan Architectural History Project, Regional Oral History Office.

The Archives of the California Historical Society, San Francisco.

The California Polytechnic State University, San Luis Obispo: Papers of Julia Morgan.

The Archives of the Hearst San Simeon State Historical Monument, San Simeon.

INDEX

Page numerals in *italics* refer to illustrations.